MW01231033

Eliminate Stress

How to Master Your Emotions and Declutter Your Mind. A Guide to Stop Worrying. Habits to Relieve Anxiety and Eliminate Negative Thinking.

Table of Contents

Introduction 5

Chapter 1: Eliminate Stress 8

Chapter 2: Master Your Emotions 29

Chapter 3: Declutter Your Mind 50

Chapter 4: Stop Worrying 69

Chapter 5: New Habits 88

Chapter 6: Relieve Anxiety 107

Chapter 7 - Eliminate Negative Thinking 130

Conclusion 148

Introduction

Congratulations on purchasing *Eliminate Stress* and thank you for doing so.

I'm so stressed out! That's a sentence we hear all too often these days. Looking at the amount of pressure that we must deal with each day, it's easy to see why. Managing stress is becoming increasingly more difficult as the pressures and responsibilities start to pile up, and to make matters worse, most of us are walking around out there without a clue how to properly manage the emotions that we feel. Unregulated stressful emotions might not seem like such a big deal, but it matters more than you think. It is a *VERY* big deal, and if you keep going on the way that you are, it won't be long before stress starts morphing into anxiety, and anxiety into depression. The impact of modern-day stress is very real and it is time that we took it seriously before it gets to the point where it becomes more than we can handle.

The statistics relating to stress are alarming. Americans, as it turns out, are the most stressed-out people in the world, one research reveals. The survey results were part of the Gallup poll conducted annually and more than

150,000 participants from all over the world took part in the survey. The statistics are not alarming for America alone. Globally, feeling stressed in the workplace is on the rise, with 6 out of 10 employees in some of the world's major economics admitting that they feel increasingly stressed at work. Employees in China had the highest level of workplace stress, at a staggering 86%, while 91% of Australians (adults) report that they feel stressed in at least one major area of their lives. Back in 2007 and 2008, approximately 442,000 adults who worked in the UK believed that they were becoming ill from work-related stress. The World Health Organization reports that depression is one of the leading causes of disability globally.

Clearly, stress is not to be taken lightly. *Eliminate Stress* is going to cover some major areas related to stress, including how to master your emotions, declutter your mind, and eliminate negative thinking. Everything you need to know and more about how to start eliminating (or at the very least try to minimize it) stress and to stop worrying about the things you cannot control.

There are plenty of books on this subject on the market, thanks again for choosing this one! Every effort was made to ensure it is full of as much useful information as possible, please enjoy!

Chapter 1: Eliminate Stress

Stress is an inevitable part of life. Responsibilities, commitments, financial obligations, career obligations, trying to find a balance between work and personal life. We live in very stressful times indeed. There seem to be more factors out there these days that trigger stress more than ever, with one study claiming that more than half of Americans are dealing with some form of moderate stress. Not all forms of stress are bad, though.

Certain forms of stress can keep you alert and focused on what you need to do. In the right doses, stress can give you the extra push you need to get things done. No one is immune to stress. Everyone experiences it. The only difference is the *way* the symptoms affect you physically since everyone has their stress coping mechanisms.

The Many Stressful Sources

Stress has become such a common occurrence that a lot of us don't remember what it was like to live stress-free anymore. It is not uncommon these days for many to experience stress daily. Some people have found ways to regulate their stress and keep it under control, while others quickly unravel and go off the deep end as soon as they begin to feel the first signs of stress. But where does it all come from? Why do we experience it to such a degree?

Stress could be due to any number of factors, some of which include:

- **Being Fatigued and Overworked -** Stress is a silent killer, and nowhere is this example perfectly illustrated than when we are being overworked. Being overworked can take a tremendous toll on the body mentally and physically. We may not feel it while we're working, but when it hits you, it hits hard. One day you wake up and realize you're dealing with a bad case of fatigued, completely exhausted and burned out because you've been overworked for far too long.

- **Trying to Survive -** Our instinct is to survive when we're faced with any kind of physical danger. The fight or flight response kicks in when triggered by what the brain perceives as any kind of danger, and the body begins churning out the adrenalin you need to give you the required energy and strength to get yourself out of that dangerous situation. When we're confronted, there are only two ways we will choose to respond. We will either stand our ground and confront the danger (fight) or we will flee (flight). However, with the hectic lifestyles, we lead today, almost everything could be perceived as "danger" when those factors happen to trigger our anxiety. If your job makes you anxious, your fight or flight response is unknowingly triggered and you could spend almost an entire day with high levels of adrenalin and cortisol in your body. The human body was not meant to store these hormones for prolonged periods and doing so could have long-term damaging effects physically.

- **Your Stressful Environment** - The environment you spend the most time in is going to have the biggest influence on your psyche. If you're constantly in a fast-paced, high-pressured, on-the-go stressful environment, it is likely to be one of your triggers. Bad weather, horrible traffic conditions, a chaotic office space, your boss breathing down your neck over the deadline that is looming, the pressure to perform well in school, trying to balance personal and professional expectations, there's a lot that could be contributing to your stress. Except that we've become so used to our environment we don't even notice it anymore.

- **What's Happening Within You -** Do you worry a lot? Someone for no apparent or concrete reason? Worrying too much is a trigger, especially when you're getting worked up over situations that may be out of your control. Some people are so accustomed to feeling stressed all the time that their subconscious mind has started *looking for reasons* to be stressed out.

Defining What Stress Is

When your body is reacting to the changes it experiences, stress is the way it responds to that adjustment period. Your body's reaction is triggered when we experience any emotional, physical, or mental stress. The changes are not necessarily negative either. Positive life changes could be potential triggers too, like when there's a new baby in the house or taking on the responsibility of a mortgage once you've bought your first home. Stress is absolutely a normal emotion, one that each one of us is bound to encounter several times over the span of our lives. In small doses, they're nothing to worry about. When it's chronic, ongoing, and intense, however, it could have serious mental and physical consequences.

Everyone experiences stress very differently. The way one person responds or reacts to the situation might not be the same as another. One person might struggle when they are under pressure, while another might thrive. Generally, we have different ways that we respond to the stimuli we encounter. You might think public speaking is a terrifying, anxiety-ridden episode while someone else might love the attention of being in the spotlight.

While it can cause a lot of problems, stress is not classified as a mental health condition. Not technically, at least unless it advances towards anxiety and depression. It may not fall within the mental health troubles category, but stress needs to be addressed before it becomes a catalyst for even more several mental health conditions like anxiety and depression. We must learn to recognize the signs and symptoms before it reaches the stage where it's too late to do anything.

The Good vs The Bad

Feeling short bursts of stress that don't last long is nothing to be alarmed about. Short-term stress, like when you have to host a meeting or submit your report on time before the deadline, usually goes away once the situation is over. These stressors are short-lived, and it is how your body gets itself through what it thinks is a tough situation. Once the moment has passed, everything goes back to what it was and you're calm again. These are good-stress, triggering short bursts of adrenalin that supply you with the attention and focus you need to get it done and over with.

Bad stress, however, is something else altogether. Negative emotions are very stressful, and it is certainly no fun to feel worried, angry, frustrated or scared all the time. These are bad stressors ad since they tend to linger for the long-haul unless you do something about it, they can cause some serious damage in the process. Everyone is affected by stress differently, and some triggers that might be the cause of long-term bad stress include the following:

- Working long hours or being overworked
- Losing your job
- Getting bullied or ridiculed
- Relationship or marriage problems
- Experiencing a divorce or breakup
- Experiencing the death of a loved one
- Moving to a new place or a new job
- A busy schedule that leaves you feeling like you have no time for yourself
- Family problems
- Difficulties at work or at school

Spotting the Symptoms
Facing continuous challenges, going through a series of bad days or bad episodes with no time for relaxation or any kind of relief in between makes us susceptible and vulnerable to stress. When this happens, the tension we feel starts to build-up. Our bodies have an in-built stress response in our autonomic nervous system which triggers the necessary physiological changes that allow our bodies to overcome

these stressful episodes. That's the fight or flight response again, which is always activated in the event of a perceived emergency. The term fight or flight first started going around sometime in the 1920s as the first part of involuntary general adaptation syndrome. The alternative to the fight or flight response is the relaxation response that the body has. This is known as the recovery period between fight or flight response and it is the body's way of normalizing its functions. This happens between 20 to 60 minutes after the perceived threat disappears.

The fight-or-flight response is a reaction to stress and this is a reaction that most likely evolved out of the survival needs from our early ancestors who lived in dangerous times. For example, prehistoric cavemen were in constant danger of animals. One minute they might be lighting a fire and the next minute, there's a stampede coming their way full of mammoths. The human design then kicks in and we have a full surge of energy and strength to quickly respond to the threat by removing ourselves from danger and increasing our chances of survival. However, when this response is chronically present and remains active because of the prolonged stressful periods we endure, it can cause significant wear and tear on our bodies, physically and emotionally.

When the stressful moments experienced are ongoing, the condition I then called *distress*. During this stage, the body's equilibrium is disrupted, which then leads to health problems and physical symptoms, including:

- Chronic headaches
- Digestive issues
- High blood pressure
- Sexual dysfunction
- Emotional turmoil
- Chest pains
- Muscular aches and pains
- Difficulty breathing during the onset of a panic attack
- Heart diseases
- Cancer
- Liver cirrhosis
- Difficulty sleeping at night (insomnia)
- Chronic fatigue no matter how much rest you've had
- Indigestion
- Dizziness

- Generally feeling like you're "out of it" or "under the weather"
- Acid reflux
- Exhaustion
- Sweaty and cold palms
- Weight loss or weight gain
- Physically shaking or trembling when you're feeling stressed or anxious

Areas of the body affected by stress

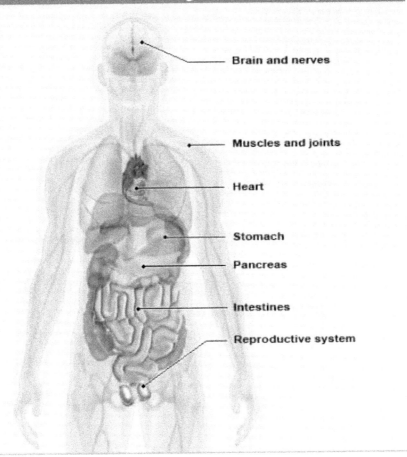

The warning signs that you might be experiencing what is known as "stress overload" are:

- Chronic worry that never seems to go away no matter what you do
- Frequent panic attacks
- Constantly feeling pressured throughout the day for several days in a row
- Overeating
- Turning to unhealthy habits like alcohol or drugs to help you "cope" with your stress
- Smoking
- Withdrawing from your family and friends

Stress is not meant to linger for too long. Our bodies were not built to cope with it and once it reaches the chronic stage, it might be too late if the damaging effects inflicted are already permanent. Chronic stress inflicts emotional symptoms too, and the signs to watch out for include:

- Anxiety

- Being moody
- Feeling restless
- Irritability
- Depression, unhappiness, and sadness
- Diminished motivation

When you feel like the stress has become more than you can handle, it is time to consider seeking help from a professional or specialist. Talk to your regular doctor or general practitioner about the symptoms that you're feeling. They may be able to refer you to a mental health professional who will have the right resources and tools to help you.

Understanding Emotional and Physical Stress

It's hard to think clearly. You're feeling scattered and forgetful. Every day feels like another day of misery where nothing seems to go right. Some studies reveal that those who reportedly undergo a lot of stress feel tired all the time and less productive as their day progresses. They are also a lot more likely to develop unhealthy coping mechanisms like bingeing on fast food or junk food, drinking, and smoking, according to the experts in these studies. Unfortunately, they fail to realize that indulging in such unhealthy coping mechanisms will only lead to *more* stress, rather than be of any help coping with it.

The Impact of Modern Day Stress

Modern life is a lot more convenient today than it ever was before. As we continue to progress forward, technology only makes life easier, more efficient and moves it along at a faster pace. There is an app for everything these days, and most of the answers we seek are only a few clicks away on the world wide web. So why are we more stressed today than we have ever been? 40 million American adults are affected today by anxiety, with millions more battling all sorts of depression-relation conditions. The National Institute of Mental Health estimates that at least 18% of adults are dealing with some mental illness, and most adults find themselves dealing with more stress than they can handle during their prime productive and child-rearing years.

As convenient as modern-day living has become, it also seems to be the source of a lot of our stress. Especially the bad stress, often a result of emotional situations more so than anything else. Our high-powered, high-pressured, fast-paced and on-the-go lifestyles leave us feeling drained and exhausted physically and mentally. By the time you're done with everything you need to do, all you want to do is go to bed. But then, you dread waking up in the morning because you know you have to repeat the same cycle over again. It seems never-ending, and it's wearing you down. It probably explains why so many of us look forward to the weekend as a short break from the 9 to 5 routine. Even when you go to bed at night, you wake up the next day feeling exhausted. You went to bed stressed, and you woke up the next morning feeling stressed and like you barely got any sleep at all.

Modern-day stress has weakened us considerably, and it is the root cause of a lot of our health problems these days. With too much cortisol flowing through our bodies, we eventually become weak. As a result, we begin to develop a myriad of other health conditions thanks to the weaker immune system we have, including:

- Asthma
- Respiratory problems
- Tuberculosis

- Different types of allergies
- Peptic ulcers
- Diabetes mellitus
- Hyperthyroidism
- Migraines and severe headaches
- Arthritis
- Rheumatism
- Various skin disorders and problems

With so much to do and so many stimuli coming at us from all different directions, being under a lot of stress can lead to a lot of bad decisions and poor judgment. Stress has made us so exhausted that we can't think clearly anymore, and in our haste to get it over and done with, we don't evaluate all our options and try to decide on the best course of action. The more bad decisions we make, the worse our productivity and motivation become. The quality of work we produce in our careers starts to slip, and we can no longer produce the same results we did in the past.

Experiencing a mental breakdown in modern times is so common it doesn't surprise us anymore. But very rarely do we make the connection to stress is one of the main contributing factors to our mental breakdown.

Experiencing extreme anxiety and depression happens to such an extreme that anyone going through it begins to experience what is referred to as disassociation. They end up being so crippled by their condition they can no longer function regularly. Stress and anxiety can cause us to behave differently than we normally would and the thing is, we normally wouldn't notice it because these seem like normal conditions other people go through as well. When we have anxiety and stress, we tend to overdo the things that are actually a normal habit.

Post Traumatic Stress Disorder (PTSD) is when stress is taken to the extreme in the aftermath of a traumatic incident or accident. PTSD could happen if you experienced a severe psychological shock too. Those who struggle with PTSD find it difficult to sleep and even when they do, they are haunted and continue to be traumatized by the memory of what left a deep scare on them. PTSD is not a condition that should be taken lightly since it can have rather severe consequences on your ability to function normally. Interacting with the people you normally do could go from effortless to an ordeal when dealing with PTSD.

Stress Management Matters

Going through a lot of stress is putting your body and your mind through the wringer. It will be a miraculous feat if you can emerge on the other side of prolonged stress without sustaining any damage. Stress will rob you of your happiness and, in extreme cases, your will to live and stress management is the only way to work on reclaiming your life once again so you're not at the mercy of your emotions. Learning to manage your stress means taking a more active approach in finding positive habits to counteract the negative emotions that you feel. Doing the things you love to do, for example, is one way of managing your stress and a way to channel all those pent up emotions through an activity that you enjoy.

Stress management techniques would depend on what works best for you. The main idea is to find ways to manage it since you may not be able to get rid of it entirely. Management and coping mechanisms are about taking preventative measures to keep your stress from escalating out of control. We need to accept the fact that stress is an unavoidable part of life, and the next best thing we can do is to try and work on not feeling these emotions every day. Instead of feeling stressed seven days a week, the right management techniques can help you bring it down to two or three days a week. One common misconception is the false belief that we "can't do anything about stress". That is not true at all. *You* are still the one who is in control. *You* are the one who makes the final decision. *You* still get to decide how you choose to handle the situation. Stress can make you feel powerless, but you never are and it is important that you start believing that right now.

Boosting Resilience

Your resilience is how well you're able to bounce back and deal with the challenges that life tosses your way. Your resilience could mean the difference between success and failure. Between staying calm in the face of pressure and completely losing your cool. Resilience is the one that keeps your positive outlook when you're faced with difficulties, and ultimately, resilience is the difference between success and failure. Some people are naturally resilient, while others need to develop ways of boosting this quality within themselves. Fostering resilience is your first self-improvement technique as you work to overcome your stress, and this is what you can do to boost your resilience:

- **Identify Your Sense of Purpose -** What do you want out of life. Are you going to let your negative emotions and thoughts define who you are and dictate what your life should be? Or do you want more out of this one life that you have to live? The decision is yours to be as positive or as negative as you want to be in the face of stress. Choosing the former is much easier when you've identified a sense of purpose, something you can use as an anchor that keeps you rooted and wavering so your stress will never get the best of you.

- **Develop Positive Beliefs -** Start believing in yourself. Believe in your abilities. Believe that this stressful period is not going to last forever. The storm will pass and you need to believe you are strong enough to stick it out. Focus on your strengths and all the other trials you've managed to overcome before. You got through those and you are much stronger because of it. You can certainly get through anything with the right attitude and positive beliefs backing you up.

- **Have a Strong Support System -** Having people you trust to confide in makes a world of difference. Knowing you have a support system is there reminds you that you're not alone. When you find your motivation diminishing, this support system can be the strength you need to claw your way up again. Talking about your troubles and confiding in your family and loved ones won't make your problems go away, but it will make you feel much better.

- **Be Willing to Embrace Change -** Because it is another part of life that is inevitable. Disliking it or trying to avoid it is not going to keep you protected from the changes in life that will happen. You're only encouraging your negative thinking patterns that trigger your stress by trying to run away from change. Embrace it, welcome it, and see it as a learning opportunity. Shift your perspective and you'll change your stress levels too when you're not as alarmed by the change you have to face.

- **Become a Problem Solver** - There's a sense of pride and accomplishment that comes with knowing you can solve almost any conundrum you find yourself faced with. Research reveals that those with problem-solving skills find that they can cope much better with the challenges they face. Each time you're confronted with a problem, instead of giving in to your first instinct to stress and panic, take a few deep breaths and try to make a list of what you can do to resolve the problem at hand. Making this list gives you something to focus on other than what is triggering your stress. Becoming a problem-solver by habit will eventually turn you into someone who can remain unfazed in almost any difficult situation. Instead of churning out cortisol, your mind will be churning out new ideas and solutions. Much better for your health in the long run.

Chapter 2: Master Your Emotions

They rule our lives. They can be a force so powerful that when they take over, we give in to impulsive reactions and hasty decisions. A lot of the decisions that we make are based on the emotions we feel. We decide based on how happy, sad, angry, or frustrated we're feeling at the time. When you're feeling happy, for example, you're more likely to take a chance and seize an opportunity with an open mind. When you're miserable, everything feels pointless and you wonder why we bother doing anything at all when nothing seems to go right anyway. So you decide not to take any action since you don't see the point of it. We even choose the hobbies and activities we want to partake in based on the emotions that they make us feel.

Defining These Powerful Emotions

Definitions of emotions have shifted and changed over time as several researchers have attempted to accurately define what emotions are. Researchers like Paul Eckman believes that universally, we all experience six basic types of emotions that goes across cultures. No matter who you are or where you may come from, the six emotions that are universally experienced by everyone in the world are happiness, anger, fear, sadness, disgust, and surprise. Sometime in 1999, Eckman decided to expand his list and branch out from the six basic emotions to include several emotions. These were now classified as basic emotions too. The list then included satisfaction, shame, embarrassment, contempt, pride, amusement, and excitement.

Around the 1980s, another American psychologist, Professor Robert Plutchik, introduced what is known as the "Wheel of Emotions", which was a system used to classify emotions. Plutchik's model showed how the various emotions we experienced could sometimes be combined together, and he went on to propose that there were primarily eight different emotional dimensions that we experienced. Plutchik believed that emotions could be combined, like the way an artist mixes several paint colors together to create new colors. When they were combined, they could create a whole host of new other emotions to be experienced. Happiness, for example, could be combined with anticipation and the resulting emotion could be excitement.

Image Source: _Pinterest_

Don and Sandra E. Hockenbury, authors of *Discovering Psychology,* define emotions as a complex psychological state. According to the authors, this psychological state involves some very distinctive components. Three of them, to be exact, which are *the expressive response, the*

experience we undergo subjectively, the physiological response that is invoked.

The three key elements that lead to our best understanding of emotions:

- The subjective experience
- The physiological response
- The behavioral response

Image Source: <u>Verywell Mind</u>

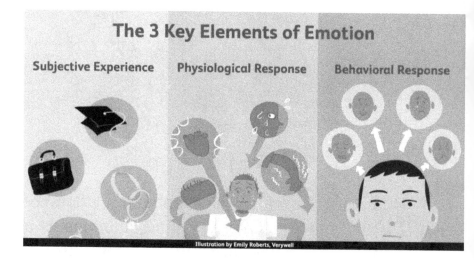

Defining the Subjective Experience

Several experts like Plutchik and Eckman for example, believe in the basic universal emotions that we all experience. We have broad labels for the range of emotions we feel, like "*angry*", "*happy*", "*good*", or "*sad*", but *the way we experience* these emotions is subjective. There are a lot of multi-dimensional factors that get involved. Take anger, for example. Not all anger is the same, and the intensity at which you experience this emotion could be anywhere from mild annoyance to perhaps full-on blind rage.

The subjectivity of this concept is also partly because we don't necessarily experience these emotions in its purest form. It is common to experience a range of mixed emotions. When you're moving to a new city or starting a new job, it is possible that you're feeling happy and nervous at the same time. When you're about to have a baby, you could experience both joy and anxiety simultaneously. Not everyone experiences the same emotions with the same level of intensity either.

Defining the Physiological Response
When your heart palpitates with fear and your stomach lurches from anxiety, that's the moment you realize what a strong physical reaction your emotions can cause. The *Cannon-*

Bard Theory of Emotion explains this phenomenon. Philip Bard and Walter Cannon in their Cannon-Bard theory of emotion, which is sometimes referred to as the Thalamic theory of emotion too, explains that when we simultaneously feel strong emotions *and* have a physiological response at the same time, these could manifest themselves physically such as through trembling, a tension in the muscles or even sweating. That's the body's autonomic nervous system at work and the reason why some situations tend to trigger the fight or flight response within us. It's because of these autonomic responses.

Our body's autonomic nervous system is the one that controls our involuntary responses, while the sympathetic nervous system controls our inbuilt flight or flight response. Any emotion that you experience is going to affect your body and your mind. Your brain is the organ in your body responsible for creating these emotions. Specifically, the limbic brain. When someone cuts in front of you as you're waiting in line, the messages that get sent to the limbic structure tell your brain that you should feel annoyed or angry about this.

Defining the Behavioral Response

This is where the actual expression of emotions take place. We spend a great deal of time trying to interpret the emotions of the people around us, but we don't spend nearly as much time trying to make sense of the emotions we feel. The ability to accurately interpret and understand emotional expression is what psychologists refer to as *emotional intelligence,* and they have a major role to play in our body language expression overall.

Emotions Are *Not* Your Moods

The two terms are used interchangeably so often that we forget emotions and moods are *not the same things.* An emotion is usually a short-lived episode, but an intense one. When we experience an intense emotion, it is likely there was an identifiable and definite trigger that caused the reaction. Your moods, on the other hand, are a milder form of the emotions we feel but they tend to last a lot longer. It can sometimes be hard to pinpoint what caused the specific mood you feel, like when you feel gloomy for days but you have no idea why.

The Way We're Impacted By the Emotions We Feel

Every emotion that you feel matters. Whether its happiness, anger, sadness, anxieties, worries, depression, joy or jubilation, *every* single one of your emotions matter and you should never suppress them, no matter what anyone tries to tell you. Emotions are a part of who we are, and suppressing them would be like suppressing part of yourself. It is unnatural, and given how emotions have a big impact on the way we feel about ourselves and our lives, no good can ever come out of suppressing them. Especially your negative emotions.

Managing your negative emotions can be a complex idea to grasp. You're not trying to avoid these emotions altogether or trying to let them wreak havoc, but at the same time, you can't deny or suppress them either. Negative emotions are a lot more powerful than their positive counterparts and have been directly linked to numerous health-related problems already. Being in a state of frequent emotional turmoil can lead to stress, which as we all know, is never good for the body. The elevated cortisol levels, adrenaline pumping through our veins, these are referred to as "stress hormones", and when they course through our bodies, they're pumping us up to react in a way that is quick and strong. Anger that is left unmanaged could lead to the destruction of relationships when hurtful words are exchanged in the heat of the moment.

Trying to find a way to manage the negative emotions you feel has a lot to do with embracing the fact that you feel them, understanding why you feel them, give yourself enough time to work through them, and then let go instead of holding on to them and move forward from there. Negative emotions like stress, for example, can have a tremendously negative impact on our bodies, not just physically, but emotionally too. On an emotional level, feeling stress and other negative emotions can result in irritability, feeling depressed and worthless, loss of purpose in life and loneliness. We start to feel isolated like nobody understands what we're going through, we become withdrawn, feel a sense of loneliness and eventually start to feel depressed because of all the imagined worries we are carrying about on our shoulders. It is *not the norm* to be living in a constant state of stress. You may think that it can't be helped, or that's just how your life is and stress is a part of it, but this is not how we were meant to live. That's the kind of impact negative emotions can have on our minds.

The problem with negative emotions is they have a much greater impact on us *because* we try so hard to avoid them. Let's face it, these emotions make us uncomfortable, and if we could we would prefer not to experience them at all. Unfortunately, that's not possible but if we don't learn how to properly cope with them, there's a greater possibility that the impact these emotions leave on us could be worse. On a physical level, certain emotions can leave an impact that includes side effects like weight gain, insomnia, chronic fatigue and muscular aches Yet, many people tend to brush it off and not think twice about the connection between these symptoms and emotions, not realizing how this behavior pattern and way of thinking of is having damaging effects to their health. Chronic illnesses like depression have been linked to poor mental health, which is often directly related to poor regulation of emotions. Experiencing these unhealthy emotions over a long term period then leads to chronic illnesses, such as heart disease, diabetes, and even a stroke.

Emotions exist to tell us what is going on. It is our body's way of communicating with us, to indicate that something may need to change. If you've been feeling miserable for days, that's obviously a very clear sign that something is not right and you need to do something about it. They motivate us to make a change for the better. Let's look at these other examples of how we are impacted by the emotions that we feel:

- **The Impact on Your Productivity -** When we're happy, we're naturally motivated to do more regardless of what the task is. Economists at the University of Warwick discovered in a study that when employees were happy, it resulted in a 12% spike in their productivity levels at the office. A flow of happy emotions also means we are less likely to experience any side effects or symptoms that are invoked by negative emotions, such as frequent headaches, higher blood pressure, gastritis issues and more, all of which tend to affect productivity levels.

- **The Impact on Your Health -** According to a 2013 article published in the *Primary Care Companion for CNS Disorders*, experiencing unhealthy emotions over a long term period leads to chronic illnesses, such as heart disease, diabetes, and even a stroke.

How to Change Your Emotions

Our brain stores the experiences we undergo like the way your computer stores your files. To recall a specific experience, your mind needs to go back and access these files where the information is stored. The memories we have are selective, meaning that we choose to remember *what* we want to remember based on the emotions we feel. When we're feeling angry, our selective memory may begin recalling all the similar situations in the past that made us feel angry too. In doing so, we end up feeding into the existing anger we have, becoming even angrier in the process, intensifying the emotions we feel. Our emotions shift and change based on the triggers we're exposed to and the memories we recall. So how do we use this information to help change our emotions?

The best strategy to adopt would be to first embrace the emotions we feel (both good and bad), and secondly engage in specific activities that help us counterbalance the effects of these emotions so there is a more balanced, authentic approach to it:

- **Teach** - Change begins with self-awareness and this relies heavily on our ability to teach ourselves to accept the way our emotions impact our mind and body. With acceptance comes understanding and a better ability to interpret what messages our body is trying to send us through these emotions.

- **Express** - Allowing the expression of these emotions is part of the acceptance process. When you need to, take a moment to freely express the emotions that you feel the need to release. Let it out, take a deep breath, get it off your chest and feel better. Be mindful of what emotions trouble you the most and release them. Take a moment whenever you need to find a quiet space away from everyone else where you can freely express all the emotions you feel you need to let out. Once you feel much better, you can rejoin the rest of the world again.

- **Befriend** - Practice self-compassion and tolerance for the way that you feel. Your emotions are part of who you are, and you have a right to feel them in the unique way you do. When you're experiencing a negative emotion, being too hard on yourself is only going to increase the stress and frustration you feel. Instead, choose to befriend your emotions. Acknowledge they exist and don't beat yourself up over it. We were not meant to experience happy emotions alone, there must be a balance in life. The way you approach both the good *and* bad feelings in life will determine how much it affects you.

- **Reframe Your Thoughts** - Change is something that rarely ever comes easy. When you're trying to change what is part of your personality, the very thing that makes you human, and something that has been part of your life for so long, it's going to be even more of a challenge. Emotions can get the best of you, which is why learning to deliberately slow down your thoughts and emotions can go a long way towards helping you learn how to

42

control and effectively deal with them. Practice slowing your thoughts down, to make sure that you are in control at every step of the way. Reframe the way you think about your negative emotions. Instead of seeing them as the enemy, see them as an experience that you can learn something from.

- **The Positive/Negative Ration** - According to research, a <u>3-to-1 positive vs negative ratio</u> of emotions is the most beneficial for our happiness in the long run. This means you need to increase the positive experiences in your life so you've got a lot more happy memories to focus on. The ratio encourages spend a longer period of time savoring the happy memories to increase the time that we spend feeling authentically good about ourselves.

- **Purposely Choose to Do What Makes You Happiest** - Happiness is a choice, but it is a choice that we forget is within our control. Those who struggle with their emotions are often unhappier than most, which makes it very hard to hold onto any kind of happiness. To find balance in your emotions, the best way to take is to do something that makes you happy. When you find yourself in an emotional situation and you're struggling to get a hold of yourself, walk away and choose instead to do something that makes you happy. Each time you actively try to engage in an activity that brings you joy, you'll find your negative emotions ebbing away quicker with each effort you make.

- **Practice Mindfulness Meditation** - It's easy to dismiss meditation and think that it isn't going to change anything when you're feeling so down in the dumps nothing seems to make a difference anymore. But think about this for a minute: *Meditation is a practice which has been around for decades*, and there's a very good reason why – because it *works*. It's effective at invoking feelings of calm and relaxation, at teaching you how to breathe so you can better control your panic attacks, and meditation helps you mindfully quiet and calm your thoughts

44

so you can get your anxieties and panic attacks under control.

- **Don't Be Afraid to Act** - Sometimes you need to take action to change your emotions for the better. Forcing your emotions towards a positive direction is something you need to do when the situation calls for it. Like when you have been procrastinating on a task for too long and you're now forced to take action as the deadline looms closer. Forcing yourself to act is taking an active role in changing the emotions you feel. From procrastination, you're slowly inching your way towards motivation. Likewise when you're feeling anger, forcing yourself to turn your emotions around by focusing on something that makes you feel good is how you give yourself the push you need to change your emotions.

- **Create Your Triggers** - If your negative emotions can be triggered, it stands to reason that your positive ones can too. If you can't think of any specific triggers that make you feel good, go ahead and create your own. Listen to music that makes you feel good. Visualize mental images that infuse you with positive emotions. Think about your dreams and the life you want for yourself. Recall some of the happiest moments in your life and immerse yourself in the memories. If certain activities trigger your feel-good emotions, go ahead and do them. When you can't think of triggers, it's okay to create your own. Just be sure to avoid the wrong kind of triggers, since you don't want to risk aggravating the wrong emotions.

- **Envision the Best Version of Yourself -** We've all imagined the kind of person we want to be and the kind of life we want to have on more than one occasion. This visualization exercise where you're envisioning the best version of yourself is now going to be used as a tool to change your emotions. Visualization is an empowering method which can help to motivate you to stay on track, and it is a great "muscle strengthening exercise" to work your subconscious with as you shape it to become what you want. Picture yourself accomplishing your goals or achieving success in everything that you do. Picture in your mind's eye only good outcomes of what it is that you desire. See that picture so clearly in such detail that you believe it is real.

- **Wear Your Gratitude Like A Coat -** *"If you wear your gratitude like a cloak, it will feed every corner of your life" - Rumi.* The 13-th century poet's wisdom is an insightful tool about what gratitude can do to turn your emotions around. When you're feeling so grateful for all the good things you have in your life, it's downright impossible to feel like a victim. Even in the hardest circumstances, there is something to be grateful for if you look hard enough. When you've had a bad day and it feels like nothing has gone right, you can still be grateful to have the love of family waiting for you to come home. Find your reason to be grateful and your whole outlook will change.

- **Situational Selection** - If you know a situation is going to trigger an emotional response from you, avoid it at all costs. Do your best to stay away from it, especially if you know ahead of time that it's coming. Let's look at this example, where you know getting caught in traffic causes a lot of negative emotions, try to leave 10 or 15 minutes earlier from your home to avoid the unnecessary burden of dealing with these emotions, which are likely going to affect your mood for the rest of the day. If you can't avoid the situation entirely, make adjustments and modifications to it so you still maintain the upper hand over your emotions. Find solutions to minimize the emotions you're trying to avoid, there's always a solution to every problem, you just have to spend enough time thinking about it and planning for it. These modifications need to be based on the kind of emotion you're trying to deal with or minimize. Like disappointment, for example. If you were trying to avoid disappointment over missing a movie you've been waiting to watch for so long, trying to arrange your schedule so all your affairs are in order and your schedule is kept as clear as possible on the day of the movie premiere. Even if something last minute comes up, you'll still have time to deal with it because you've adjusted your schedule and kept it clear of any pressing or urgent matters.

Chapter 3: Declutter Your Mind

Do you ever feel like if you were to look inside your brain, you would see a big, chaotic, messy pile of disorganized thoughts? When it feels like your brain is being hit left, right and center by a never-ending stream of thoughts and stimuli, it feels like your brain is in serious overdrive mode all the time. Hence, the stress that you feel. Your brain is sending you an SOS signal, waving a red flag frantically hoping you'll read the signs and free your mind. Imagine that your mind is like the closets and cabinets you have in your home. You spring clean those once in a while because you know that if you don't, the mess is going to build up and start overflowing. Well, your mind works the same way. We may not be able to physically see it, but we can *feel* when our minds are in serious need of some decluttering. Except instead of getting rid of physical items, what you're going to do this time is clear out the excess, non-essential baggage in the form of unhelpful and unnecessary thoughts. Clear them out and your mind will be free to focus on staying productive and motivated.

Say the word "clutter" and most of us immediately think about the physical clutter in our immediate environment. Unless someone points it out, you probably might not have thought about the fact that your mind is capable of hoarding habits too. You'll know when this is happening when you notice the following signs:

- You're ruminating too much
- You spend too much time focusing on negativity
- You're obsessing about what is beyond your control
- You have a hard time letting go of negativity
- You have a hard time letting go of your anger and resentment
- You have a hard time letting go of sadness and any unpleasant emotion that is weighing you down
- Your mental to-do checklist has a lot of unfulfilled goals and dreams on it
- You're easily distracted by your external circumstances
- New sensory stimuli and input makes you feel overwhelmed too easily

Unfortunately, no good can ever come out of a cluttered mind. You're using up too much mental energy and wasting a lot of precious time. A cluttered mind leads to disorganization, distraction, confusion, and makes it hard for you to make productive decisions, maintain a clear focus, sort out your priorities and in general, be productive. Dealing with a cluttered mind is not something to be taken lightly. Let it go on for long enough and you'll eventually lose touch with your present. You'll feel disconnected with yourself and your environment until finally, you begin losing touch with the relationships you have too. It can feel like you're walking around in an unfocused daze, unhappy and stressed, not knowing what you're doing with your life and why.

The only solution to this conundrum is to declutter your mind. The mental habits that you have right now could be stopping you from achieving your full potential. You must declutter to build the mental toughness, strength, and resilience you need to never let yourself be fazed by stress again. Once you let go of the mental baggage that is weighing you down, your mind will finally be free and so will you.

What Contributes to A Cluttered Mind?

The world we live in. That's the main reason why we've got so much clutter going on upstairs. From the moment you wake up, incoming information from social media sites, Google, news channels, content sent to you by friends and family, text messages, email notifications, everything comes at you all at once the minute you open your eyes and pick up your phone. This is a huge change from the lifestyle of several decades ago when people just woke up and enjoyed a few moments of silence before they got out of bed and began their routine. Today, the human brain is busier than it has ever been throughout history. We've turned it into a constant information-processing machine with the relentless notifications and stimuli that keep coming at us.

By the time we leave the house, arrive at work and sit down behind the computer to begin the day, we may find ourselves too mentally exhausted and overwhelmed to concentrate on our job. We're stuck and we don't know what to do about it. Even when we try to focus on our job, we're threatened by distractions all the time. A chatty colleague in the next cubicle. Phones ringing off the hook. Conversations flying back and forth. The frequent beeps of your phone, indicating a new notification has just come in. Emails that keep "dinging" in on your computer. Trying to fight it and hold onto your focus is exhausting in those conditions, even worse when you're mind is more cluttered than it should be. Outside work, a lot of factors try to pull our focus in different directions too. You're worried about paying the bills this month. You don't know if you'll be able to meet your deadline when you've got two kids to look after at home. You're considering applying for a new job but you don't know if it's a good idea. There *always* seems to be something to fret, worry, or think about. Where does it end?

When you don't give your poor, overworked brain enough time to focus on one thing at a time, you feel mentally stuck. Today, the expectation is you need to multi-task if you want to get several things done at once. But here's the thing: *Our minds were NOT built to multitask.* We're supposed to only focus on *one* thing at a time, but the pressure of juggling

54

multiple responsibilities has turned multi-tasking into an acceptable thing these days. Truth be told, multitasking is ineffective in the long-run and rather than promote better concentration, it promotes anxiety instead. When you're chasing the clock instead of focusing on what you're supposed to be doing, you get nervous, flustered and anxious when you notice you're running out of time. In the haste to meet the self- imposed time deadline you've set for yourself, your focus dissipates. Mistakes get made, crucial information gets overlooked, and you're feeling emotional from the pressure of rushing to meet your time goal so you can move onto your next task. Multitasking is counterproductive, and you're contributing to your cluttered mind when you do that.

Mess Equals Stress

It's not only negative thoughts that you have to worry about cluttering your mind. Your environment has a large part to play too. Clutter happens when two types of disorganization are present: *Situational and chronic*. The first one happens when major life events or transitions take place, like getting married, moving to a new home, having a baby, losing a loved one, starting a new job. In the hecticness of change, chaos and clutter can ensue. The latter happens when we're our disorganized external environment doesn't show signs of improvement. As the clutter gets worse, so does our emotional state. Being in a messy environment can affect our mood. The amount of clutter that's sitting in your home right now could have such a deep emotional and psychological impact, and it has a way of affecting you mentally and physically without you even knowing it. Being surrounded by disorganization makes it hard for anyone to concentrate. When it becomes impossible to have clarity in your life, you begin to question and wonder what you're doing with your life.

We have become so conditioned to a life of materialism that we genuinely believe the decisions about the purchases we make are based on careful thought and sound logic, but in all honesty, that's far from the truth. There's a classic sales quote which sums up this scenario perfectly: *"People don't buy products. What they're buying is better versions of themselves"*. The purchases that we make represent our hopes, what we believed to be true when we bought them, and what we hope it will help us achieve down the road. We make purchases in the hopes that we will finally become a happier version of ourselves, the way those ads promised. Unfortunately, when that doesn't happen, we become unhappy and the emotions we feel only aggravate the mental clutter that is already there.

Eliminating Negativity from Your Life

Harboring negative emotions is a sign that your mind is cluttered. You know it is affecting you and causing you a great deal of stress, but you find it hard to let go anyway. It begins with one thought, one feeling and before you know it, you're sliding down a very slippery slope of unhappy emotions and you don't know how to slow down anymore. Negativity puts your mind in a bad place you never want it to be in, and it can quickly strip you of any possibility of happiness. It holds you back from living your best life. The trouble is, negativity is not entirely avoidable. There will be some moments in life that are less than pleasant. To say we're never going to feel the stressful effects of negativity would be a lie. We can't always avoid them, but what you can do is learn how to process these those, assess them, and deal with them in better, healthier ways so they don't linger and clutter your mind.

Release your negativity because your cluttered mind is begging for it. Release your negativity and watch how things begin to take a turn for the better. Decluttering your mind is not just about thinking less or writing things down so you're not storing it in your head. Negativity is a large part of why you feel stress, and to eliminate that stress, you must release - *you guessed it* - negativity:

- **Love and Self-Acceptance** - This is one of the many things we struggle to do. To love and accept ourselves as we are, strengths and weaknesses and all. We're far too focused on our imperfections, forgetting that we have a lot to offer, and that focus on imperfections is cluttering your mind with all sorts of unhappy thoughts. Care a little less about what others think of you. Don't let social media dictate what constitutes perfection. Focus on the good, push your insecurities out of your mind and you'll see how it turns your life and your mind around for the better.

- **Stay Away from Negative Influences** - Is there anything in your environment that is negative? If it is, this needs to be eliminated. Yes, this includes any toxic individuals who happen to be in your life. A lot of the negativity we harbor in our minds is influenced by our external environment to a certain degree. If it isn't an influence, it's a cause. It could be your toxic work environment, or the toxic friends and family that are dragging you down emotionally and it needs to stop. Get a new job and minimize the contact you have with these toxic individuals. No good can ever come out of that relationship, and you owe it to yourself to put your happiness first.

- **Consider What You Don't Want -** This sounds easy in theory, but identifying what you want and *don't* want is not that easy. If you thought about it right now, could you list five things you know you wanted? What about five things you know for sure you *don't* want? This needs some thought, but once you've identified what you don't want in your life, it's easier to work on getting rid of it.

For example, you *don't* want to be a negative and pessimistic person forever. Once you've identified that, the next step is to think about how to make that happen. Identify what you don't want your life to be surrounded with, and then come up with several solutions as to what to do about it.

- **Resetting What Your Answer Is -** What are your default answers normally like? Positive? Or the opposite? Your first response will be "no" if by default your answers are generally negative. This pattern of thinking is indicative of someone who makes excuses. Someone who wants to avoid change, even when they know that change is going to be for their benefit. Your default answer traps you in a negative mindset and to get out of it, you'll have to switch your answers. Instead of making "no" or "I can't" as your instinctive responses, try "yes" or if you need a moment to think about it, say so.

- **Minimizing Contact with Bad News** - Since a huge source of stress comes from bad news, it only makes sense that to minimize the stress we feel, we need to minimize the contact we have with bad news too. Tragedy and strife are an inevitable part of life, but if you're looking for it, you'll always see more bad than good. There's a lot of good news that happens every day too, except that it gets overshadowed by the bad news because negativity has always been an overpowering emotion. If there's too much of it going on in your life making it hard for you to focus on positivity, minimize your contact with the sources of this news. If it's stemming from social media, cut down the time you spend on these platforms. If it's from a toxic colleague who does nothing except whine and complains all day long, minimize your interaction and avoid spending time alone with them. Resist the urge to seek out bad news, you know it's not going to do you any good.

- **Turning Your Distortions Around -** Some see the glass as half empty where others might say it is half full. All of us have cognitive distortions when it comes to the way we think. These distortions shape our perception and for some people, causes negativity. Some examples of these distortions include when you assume that everybody hates you, despite there being no proof of that. When a friend cancels on you, your mind immediately assumes you've done something wrong or they don't want to be around you. Your assumptions and predictions are distorting your reality, and you need to recognize when these distortions are taking place so you can put a stop to your thoughts. For every negative thought you have, stop and ask yourself, *"Do I have any proof of this or am I assuming/predicting?"*. Eliminating your cognitive distortions makes it easier to eventually get rid of negativity too when you learn to see the world through clearer lenses.

Organizing Your Mind

Your mental habits are the reason you're not reaching your full potential right now. You've got a busy mind and it's stopping you from doing what you need to do. That's why you feel "stuck", stressed, anxious and overwhelmed so easily. A negative mind is one of the most debilitating hindrances you can have, taking up more than its fair share of space in your mind that there is no room for anything else. Like an unwanted house guest who has overstayed their welcome, the toxic behavior must be kicked out and the first thing you need to do to organize your mind once more is to develop self-awareness about your thoughts. How do you usually talk to yourself? What do you think or believe about yourself? What you're going to do now is be on the lookout for the warning signs, like victimizing thoughts or toxic self-talk tendencies.

Organizing your mind is going to require a lot of change. Decluttering was only the first step. The harder part would be trying to change the mindset you have, switching it from negative to positive. Overcoming negativity for good is probably going to be one of the hardest challenges you might have faced in a while. Breaking out of old habits that have been around for years is never an easy or straightforward process. It takes weeks of exercising positive thought replacement, which is where you replace your bad thoughts with good ones. It will take a while before you begin to feel the visile shift from a heavy, cluttered, disorganized and chaotic mind to a mind that if happier, lighter, and feeling free.

The first few steps are going to be the hardest part, but once you've built your momentum, all you need to do is keep the ball rolling. Begin by making it your mission to accumulate more positive experiences in your life. Think about what can you do each day that is going to make you happy. The activity should make you feel good in your mind, body, and soul. It can be any activity you love to do. Going for a hike, spending time with your pets, catching up for a cup of coffee after work with a good friend, anything that makes your life today feel a little bit better. These positive activities make it easier to practice gratitude. Being grateful is the best remedy for a mind that is clouded with negativity. Actively reminding yourself of your blessings lets you see that life is not as bad as it seems, despite the stressful triggers you have in it. Everyone has their own form of stress to deal with, the difference is how you choose to handle it.

Manage your stress levels by keeping your mind organized with the following strategies:

- **Allow Yourself Time to Worry -** There's going to be something to worry about. You can't avoid worry forever, so what you're doing to do instead is to be more proactive about it. Instead of letting the worry take over your entire day, keep your mind organized by allowing yourself time to worry before you return to your other tasks. In between tasks, pick a time that works best, and schedule 5 to 10 minutes specifically for your worries. Rehash your concerns, but think about *solutions* instead of distorting those thoughts and making yourself feel worse. This keeps the worries from spinning out of control and distracting you throughout the day so you can still stay on top of everything you need to do *and* process your worries without neglecting them.

- **Logging Your Gratitude -** A new habit to develop that keeps your mind organize is to schedule time in your day again to log what you're grateful for. Keeping a journal for this purpose is great for organization, and each day make it a point to list at least five things you were grateful for today. If you've got more, even better, write them all down. This exercise makes you actively think about the good things happening in your life. That despite the difficult day you might have had, there were still moments of positivity in it that brought a smile to your face. Taking the time to count your blessings is one approach to achieving more balance in your life. It's hard to be negative and grateful at the same time.

- **Learn to Laugh Again** - If you've spent too long dwelling on negativity, you've probably forgotten when the last time you laughed was. Yet, nothing is simpler or more effective and instantaneously making you feel better and relieving the stress you feel. Laugh, and laugh hard. Be around people who make you love. Watch your favorite comedies or movies, watch comedy specials, anything that is going to get you laughing in a genuine, carefree manner. Surround your life with as much laughter in a day as you can and your stress won't stand a chance.

- **Give Yourself Permission to Unwind** - Unlike what today's world may want you to think, you *don't* have to be busy all the time. Being busy doesn't necessarily mean you're being productive. Likewise, being productive doesn't mean you need to be busy every minute of the day. Trying to do too much at once is how you clutter your mind and trigger intense stressful emotions. When you're burned out and worn out, you get even less done so give yourself permission to unwind and relax. Self-care is as important as getting things done because when your health is compromised, you get *nothing* done.

- **Talking About It** - When your mind feels like it can't take anymore, talk to someone about it. The clutter you feel mentally is a result of all the thoughts and emotions you have being squished up there together with no place to go. Let them go by getting things off your chest. Talk about it because it feels better knowing you're not alone and you've got people who care about you. Talking about it with someone you trust is could even bring an added benefit with it. You get to brainstorm solutions and you'll end up feeling much better by the end of that heart-to-heart.

Chapter 4: Stop Worrying

There are some things in life that you cannot control. Unfortunately, not everyone can accept the hard truth of that reality. They either can't accept it, or they won't. Those who resist and right against the truth are usually the ones who tend to be control freaks. They try to micromanage, attempt to force others to go along with what they want, and they're reluctant to delegate tasks. They believe that controlling everything is the only way to stop "bad things" they are so worried about from happening, and when they realize they can't force the outcome that they want, they become anxious.

No one wants to deal with the unpleasant moments in life. If we could, we'd only want to fill our lives with nothing but happy memories and fun times and fast forward over the unpleasant bits. If only it worked that way. For most people, this doesn't bother them as much. They accept that sometimes in life, not everything will go your way and that's okay. They pick themselves up and move on. For chronic worries, however, they may *know* that worrying about disasters is not going to change anything, but they choose to do it anyway. They can't help themselves. They spend all that time consumed by their worries they let other responsibilities they should be focusing on get neglected. At the end of the day, they might realize their worrying did them no good, but they'll repeat the cycle again tomorrow. That's the only way they know how to cope with the stress that comes their way.

Everyone has a unique way of reacting to stress. Some can remain cool and calm under pressure, while others let themselves get swept away in the sea of their emotions. Stress impacts us in different ways, and to overcome your worries, you need to identify what your triggers are and the way that you respond when you feel pressured. Once you've identified the pattern of behavior that emerges each time you're stressed, you can work on making the necessary adjustments and develop more effective coping strategies that will strengthen you instead of breaking you down. Stress and worries *can* be a fuel for positive change, but only if you learn to control your emotions.

Morphing from Stress to Worries and Anxieties

Most people would react to stress by trying to push it away, avoid it, or suppress it. It's not an emotion they want to deal with. That's understandable. In large quantities, stress can do all sorts of things to your body. But *why* does stress happen? Is it *always* bad? Not necessarily. Imagine yourself standing in the middle. On one side, you've got demand, and on the other, capacity. You're right in the middle of the two. The stress you feel is based on your capacity to meet demand, bridging the gap between the two. Stress is neither good nor bad. Instead, it is the way you use it that makes the difference.

The energy of stress that is felt when trying to bridge the gap between demand and capacity. When the energy overwhelms you, that's when stress turns negative. Some people are able to turn this energy into the fuel that they need to channel their focus and aligning their priorities to meet the necessary demand. When that happens, the energy of stress becomes positive. It all comes down to you and how you respond when you're faced with your stress triggers.

Stress starts off as energy, but it can quickly morph into worries the moment you allow yourself to get swallowed up by the emotions that you feel. That can steadily grow worse when your worries get bigger and bigger. Instead of feeling stressed about one problem, your mind drifts towards other issues that are not related to the present problem you face. Maybe you start worrying about what you should have done, or what you could have done, or wished you had done better on problems that are not directly related to what you're having to face right now. All your thoughts start to run together, getting jumbled up until you're not sure what you're worried about anymore. All you know is that you're feeling anxious and finding it difficult to relax.

Our ability to worry is the brain's way of protecting us from the possibilities we might have to encounter, which can be a good thing if we approach from a problem-solution perspective. When you're stuck on your worries and unable to move forward, though, it becomes a problem. That's when worries began to shift towards the anxiety spectrum as it starts to intensify. Worry is more of a mental construct whereas anxiety lingers in your body. Anxiety heightens your nervous system and when you get stuck in this state for a prolonged period, your inability to relax and calm the body down is going to be a disadvantage. Anxiety causes a lot of your body's systems to go into overdrive from the hormones that are being churned out. Your heart rate escalates, you have trouble breathing, there's a tightness in your chest, or you're shaking and trembling. We're not meant to experience these sensations for long, and when your body doesn't get the time it needs to recover and truth to normal, it's going to affect your health and wellbeing in the long run.

Despite it all, we *need* stress, anxiety, and worries in our life to a certain extent. There's a reason we're hardwired for these emotions. They serve a purpose. They give us the information we need to react in ways that ensure our survival and safety. Trying to ignore them or suppress them doesn't make them go away. They'll be there, bubbling beneath the surface, causing a serious imbalance in our mental and emotional state. Like a volcano that is waiting to erupt, all those pent up emotions will burst forth at once and it won't be pretty. However, if we learned to identify our triggers, emotions, and behavior and used it to our advantage instead, we could mobilize the stressful energy. In doing so, we effectively using this energy as fuel instead of a reason to break us down.

Who Are the Ones Who Worry?

Besides the perfectionists and control freaks, there is another personality type who is also susceptible to worries. These are the people who carry the *"What if"* syndrome with. These individuals are easily identifiable because they tend to worry about all sorts of things, even when there is no reason to worry. They walk around asking *"What if"* all the time, and create reasons to worry when reasons don't exist yet. Robert L. Leahy, author of *The Worry Cure: 7 Steps to Stop Worry from Stopping You* believes this has something to do with genetics and nurture versus non-nurture factors. Those who come from divorced families, for example, have a higher tendency by as much as 70% of developing Generalized Anxiety Disorder (GAD). Overprotective parents tend to raise children who worry too much too.

Worry could be a result of biological and environmental components too. Growing up in an environment with a lot of stress-related triggers, like watching the way your family members cope with their anxiety issues will have some influence over you if that is all you grew up around. It will be the only way you know how to cope with your anxieties too.

What Makes Us Do It?

That's the big question, isn't it? We know worrying does no good, yet we do it anyway and most of us have a hard time explaining why. For the most part, a lot of worriers react the way they do because they believe something bad could or will happen. Therefore, they let themselves believe that if they worry, they might be able to stop the bad thing from happening. To others, it might not make sense, but the mind of the worrier thinks *if you can imagine that something bad is going to happen or will happen, you need to worry about it.* They see it as a responsibility, almost.

With all the negativity and poor side effects associated with too much worry, it's hard for anyone to remember that worry can sometimes be a good thing. Despite its poor reputation, worry is still first and foremost, our basic survival mechanism. If you could learn to keep your worries under control, it wouldn't be such a bad thing anymore. But when your worries are disproportionate and affect you so deeply it's disrupting your ability to function, then something needs to be done about it and fast!

Reasons You Need to Quit Your Worry

If you wanted to, there will always be a reason to worry. *Always.* The worries will never end unless you put a stop to it. If you can visualize positive images and scenarios in your mind, like what it feels like to achieve success or see yourself accomplishing your goal, you can certainly control what triggers your worry too. What you're probably lacking right now is the motivation. You need an *incentive* as to why you should stop, and here are a few reasons to consider:

- **You Won't Change the Outcome -** You need to repeat this fact to yourself as many times as needed until the message finally sinks in. you can't change the outcome with worry. *Action* is what changes the outcome. *Solutions* change the outcome. *Proactiveness* changes the outcome. Worry does not.

- **You're Missing Out On A Lot -** If there's one important life lesson you need to take away from all this, it is that *you're missing out on a lot when you worry.* Once a moment is gone, it can never return. What's happening in your present are the treasured moments you need to be focused on. Instead of worrying about what's happened or what is *yet* to happen, focus on what *is* happening around you now. Be present and enjoy it as it is because you might regret it later if you don't. If you're busy worrying about what's going to happen next week while your child is learning to take his first steps, you're missing out on one of the most precious moments in your life as a parent and you know that's not what you want to do.

- **Life Is Short** - We don't spend nearly enough time reflecting on this. If you knew you were going to die tomorrow, what would you differently today? Would you worry less and seize the moment? You only get one life, and each moment is precious because once it's gone, it is never coming back again. Time doesn't move backward, and it certainly waits for no man. Worriers are missing out on the best part of life, which is a tremendous shame. All worriers tend to do is visualize all the things that could go wrong, fretting about things that they can't control, and completely missing out on the moments happening right in front of them. When you only get one moment to live, is it worth it spending that time unhappy and miserable?

- **You're Imagining the Worse** - Think about all the times you have spent ages worrying about the worst, most disastrous outcome you could think of. How many times did those scenarios manifest? Probably barely or never. How many times has a problem seemed so monumental to you, but when that situation or circumstance actually happens, you find that it wasn't so bad after all? Too many to count? That's what chronic and obsessive worrying will do to you. Worries exaggerate the problems in their heads, making it seem even bigger than it really is. As a result, they tend to overstress and focus on the negatives outcomes of a situation, when there is no real or concrete evidence that it will happen. Our worries are magnified by our imagination, and unless you've got absolute proof that the worst will happen, there's no point letting your imagination carry you away.

- **You're Not Being Constructive** - Fretting and predicting the possible problems of the future is not productive, generating solutions to fix those problems or prevent them, is construction. Problem-solving is good, worrying is not. Time to change that pattern of behavior.

- **You'll Find It Hard to Decide Anything** - When you worry all the time, it becomes hard for you to make a decision. Each decision seems like it would come with its own set of problems and possible negative outcomes, which causes worriers to worry even more. When they finally do end up making a decision, it may not necessarily be the right decision because their judgment has been clouded by worry.

- **You Can't See the Bright Side of Life** - Losing the ability to see the positive side of situations will increase a worrier's levels of anxiety and fear, and do nothing to help quell the overwhelming sense of worry that they feel. When chronic worrying becomes a habit, the worrier loses all ability to see the silver lining in any situation. All they can think about and focus on are the negatives and they look at life as a glass half empty environment. Eventually, it becomes almost impossible to view things positively, even when there is nothing bad to think about.

Stop Worrying About What You Can't Control

You'll be a lot happier and less stressed when you do. If you channeled that time and energy you spent worrying and used it for something more productive instead, think about what a difference it would make in your life. It's going to be a struggle in the beginning, but putting a stop to your worries is not impossible. You need the right push and the right strategies to do it:

- **Identify What Is Within Your Control** - Make the first switch by training your mind to focus on identifying what you *can* control instead. What you've been doing all this time is worrying about what was outside your control. What you're going to do now is repeatedly tell yourself *what can I control in this situation?* A simple shift in your perspective and you begin to see everything in a different light. You may not be able to stop the bad things from happening, but you can prepare for it by determining which factors you can control. Your reaction is one thing you can control, so start with that and work from there.

- **Think About Your Influence** - How much influence do you have on the people who may be involved in the situation you're worried about? You may not be able to force your desired outcome, but what you can do is try to influence or persuade others to see things from your perspective. If everyone is in agreement, you can then work together towards a viable solution. You could be the role model that sets things in motion while everyone else follows your lead. This way, at least you don't have to worry that you're all alone in this.

- **No More Feeling Sorry for Yourself** - It's the kind of thinking that is going to get you nowhere. Feeling sorry for yourself is self-destructive, and you don't need this habit in your life if you're serious about overcoming your worries and anxiety. When you spend too much time pitying yourself, you don't have time to live it to the fullest. Trade-in self-pity with an attitude of gratitude and watch your worries begin to melt away.

- **Identify What You're Afraid Of** - In any situation, ask yourself what you're afraid of the most. What would be your worst nightmare come to life in that situation? Are your predictions real and based on facts? Or is your catastrophic outcome based on assumption? Pinpointing your fears makes it easier to see if they are responsible for magnifying the emotions you feel. If your fears feel like they are something that's too much for you to manage alone, it is okay to admit that you might need help or support getting yourself through it. Make a list of your worries, identify each one of them and toss out the ones which are not viable.

- **Learn to Differentiate Problem-Solving and Rumination -** Problem-solving is always going to be the better approach to take. Ruminating and replaying past scenarios or conversations in your head as you imagine your disastrous outcomes repeatedly is never going to work. What you need to do now is identify how productive the thinking you're engaged in is. How do you find ways to minimize the impact of what you're worried about? As soon as you catch yourself ruminating and not coming up with a solution, switch channels in your brain and go back to problem-solving mode.

- **Have A Stress Plan -** Get enough sleep. Eat right. Exercise. Do activities that make you happy. Take a day off to pamper yourself. In a nutshell, *finding ways to make yourself feel good or happy* is your stress plan. You need a way to relieve yourself, everyone does.

Whenever you're feeling overwhelmed, it's not wrong to take a break and admit you need some time to care for yourself. Make it a habit to indulge in activities that feel good several times a week if you can.

- **Learn to Be Okay with Uncertainty -** There are times when the unplanned moments in life turn out to be the best thing that ever happened to you. Maybe you didn't plan to go out to the bar that night, but if your friend didn't drag you to it against your will, you might never have met your future partner. Maybe you worried about the change in management at your workplace, but several weeks later you realize how refreshing the new ideas introduced by the management could be. Uncertainty is always going to be part of what makes life go up and down, whether you like it or not. Since we can't change this fact, do the next best thing and learn to accept that uncertainty is part of yours (and everyone's) life. Accept that you don't know what the future holds, because no one does. The only difference between you and them is that they're not worrying about it. Uncertainty does not always equal the worst-case scenario outcome. Acceptance doesn't mean your worries are going to go away. It means you're *choosing* not to let it stop you from living your life.

- **You Don't Need to Be Afraid of Risks** - Sometimes you need to take risks to see change. You need to be willing to make big moves that others are not. You need to take a leap of faith if you want to make a considerable difference. That's what everyone else is doing, and if they can do it, you can too. They do have their worries and concerns, but they manage it by doing their due diligence and arming themselves with information. Knowledge is going to be your best defense against your unruly imagination. When you've got facts to fall back on, it's easier to challenge your mind when it tries to convince you otherwise.

- **You Can Handle Discomfort** - It's time to remind yourself of that fact. You're bound to have handled several moments in life when you were pushed beyond your comfort zone. You survived then, and you will keep on surviving because that's what we do as people. We adapt, we survive, we overcome discomfort and we thrive. Discomfort means you don't like what you have to do, but it does not mean you *can't* do it. You probably can. You would prefer not to, but you can.

- **Stopping the Clock** - A lot of worries are fueled by a sense of urgency. They believe they *need* to do something fast and they need to do it now. Feeling like you always have to race against the clock is the surest way to spike your stress levels. Beat the urge to race against the clock by focusing on one task at the time. Always think in moves that put you one step ahead and closer to solving the problem. Remember that you can't do anything when you're in a panicked or stressed out state. Remember that the terrible outcome you're thinking about probably won't happen. You *can* handle anything if you set your mind to it. There's no need to put a timer on everything, pace yourself and take it one step at a time.

- **It's Okay to Cry About It** - Cry when your emotions feel like they're too much to handle. Crying is not a sign of weakness, it's a way of releasing your emotions. Let it all out, don't suppress. Cry about it for a few minutes of you feel emotional. As long as you feel much better afterward, that's all that matters.

Chapter 5: New Habits

Author Stephen Covey, in his book *The 7 Habits of Highly Effective People*, explains the paradigm and principles of habits perfectly. Covey begins his book by pointing out how people are preoccupied with finding quick fixes. That people want to achieve success, but they are secretly hoping for the quickest way to do it. However, Covey points out that this is ineffective, and that real change must come from within. The change needs to begin with habits, and this is where he begins to present his seven methods of effectiveness. Here's where the paradigm of principles of these habits come in.

Paradigms are essentially your perceptions and the way you understand the world around you. By learning to base your views on the right kind of principles, you learn to work towards achieving happiness, success, and ultimately less stress. Covey encourages the readers of his book to think about paradigms as their maps. They're not a *solution,* but a *representation* of where you need to go. Like a GPS navigation system. Developing the right habits requires a shift in your paradigm so you can change the way you think. To do that, you must learn to practice awareness towards the perception of others, and decide if you're going to adopt parts of it, all of it, or disregard it entirely. These shifts in your perception could go either way (positive or negative) and it will ultimately determine the relationship you have with yourself and others. *Developing the right habits to eliminate stress is a shift in your paradigm for the better.*

Principles, on the other hand, are the natural laws that govern your growth and happiness. These could include honesty, fairness, patience, encouragement. If your paradigms are the road map you need to point you in the right direction, then the principles are the *landmarks* you use to confirm that you're on track and heading in the right direction. *Developing the right habits is your principle* and the formation of these principles is the result of a combination of skill, knowledge, and desire.

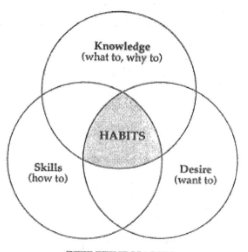

EFFECTIVE HABITS
Internalized principles and patterns of behavior

Image Source: _Achieve Goal Setting Success_

The Formation of Habit

Our brain is a powerful organ that learns your habits-whether or not you are trying to teach it. You might have noticed that the mind has a tendency to easily absorb the negative influences and bad habits faster than it does with positive, nurturing habits that require substantially more work. The formation of habit begins with two traits you must adopt if this is going to work: *Self-discipline* and *willpower*. To most people, self-discipline feels constricting but in reality, when you practice it, you began to that your life before you were disciplined, was constricting. You realize that how you spend your time, the bad habits you had and the addictions were controlling your life all this while. But when you are self-disciplined, you are more in control and you have more say of how you live your life. Your words will become actions and your actions will become habits. Your habits shape your characters and your character becomes your destiny. Practicing self-discipline is a short term pain that comes with numerous benefits in the long run.

People with self-discipline spend less time indulging in habits or behaviors that distract them from achieving their goals. They are able to make positive decisions a lot more easily, and they do not make choices based on their feelings or impulses. They make informed, rational decisions and they do not get overly stressed or upset by any changes that come their way. Self-discipline is something you cannot see or touch or taste or smell but its effects are momentous. It can transform the fat to slim, poor to rich, depressed to happy. Yes, you could say that luck plays a role but self-discipline is what prepares you to face what this lucky break may bring. Self-discipline is the ability to control your emotions and feelings to a point where it can help you overcome your weaknesses and desire to give in to temptation. People are not born with self-discipline. It is a state of mind. It is something you can learn. Once cultivated, it becomes a part of who you are, just like habits.

Willpower and self-discipline are often used interchangeably, but they are not the same. Although both qualities are essential because they work together towards helping you accomplish your goals, they have distinct differences. Willpower is the exertion when you are determined to accomplish a task. It is the level of control that an individual uses to restrain their impulses. Willpower can be short-lived and only used when the moment calls for it. Sometimes, it could be as simple as following a set of temporary rules to achieve a short-term result, like dieting or quitting smoking. In short, it is the ability to push and control yourself and your actions when needed.

Self-discipline is the key solution to getting out of our numerous nasty habits. We tend to develop many nasty mental habits that keep us from changing, from adapting, from learning and from being happy. It just makes us all miserable. Every day should be a day where good habits are practiced a little more each time. The more you work on your habits and create a routine for them, the closer you are to achieving your goals. You would naturally take some time off but if you do not take the first 7 days or first 30 days of your working on your goal, you will never create the momentum you need to drive you till you reach your desired target. The first 30 days of a goal is crucial- it not only shows people you are serious, but it also boosts your morale and the drive you need to keep you going and sustain your goals well beyond your target.

On the road to self-discipline, the more you do the right thing, the easier it will become. The more you practice willpower, the more willpower you will have. It's a simple equation. Like most habits, self-discipline is a skill that you can learn. It isn't something that you are born with. Self-discipline is what gives you more control over the way you lead your life. It also helps you change your habits and improve your skills. It helps you become an overall better person. Self-discipline is essential for personal and spiritual growth and for achieving success in all aspects of your life, especially in the formation of new habits to eliminate the stress you feel in your life.

Habits of the Mind

Our minds and our subconscious are set up to help us achieve goals that we sincerely believe are achievable. The path to achieving goals is filled with boredom, procrastination, anxiety, excuses, and difficulty. The only way to not become a victim of these traps is to arm yourself with the right habits of the mind.

Habits of the mind are best described as dispositions employed mindfully and skillfully by the emotionally intelligent, successful individuals each time they are confronted with problems. Instead of dwelling on those problems and magnifying the stress they feel, they've developed the right habits of the mind whereby they have learned to focus on solutions instead. The solution might not be apparent immediately, but that won't stop them for one, simple reason: *They are focused on the intention, rather than the behavior.* This means that when they are confronted by confusing dilemmas and uncertainty, they have learned not to let stress take the wheel. What they choose to do instead is draw from certain habits that will produce better outcomes instead.

Employing these habits requires a composite of several attitude cues, proclivities, skills, and some past experience too. When you're able to value one pattern of thought over another, it implies you're *making a choice* about which habits should be used at the right time. Mastering the habits of the mind means you've developed the ability to evaluate, modify, and reflect on what you've learned and carried those lessons with you to be applied in the future. Successful people are likely to achieve more because they have the discipline and drive to keep moving forward and to never give in or up. They have created helpful habits and they stick to them. Working hard is second nature to them. Going beyond what's needed has become a part of them and in everything that they do, they give it their all. Habits of the mind, in many respects, is about self-control. Learning to control thoughts may be one of the most difficult practices to apply.

Every time you tell yourself *"I can't do this!"*, or *"I'm not strong enough"*, you plant a seed in your mind that can grow into a self-fulfilling prophecy. Your mind is the most powerful asset you possess. Your mindset either make you or it can break you. These negative thoughts get amplified by your strong, subconscious desire and belief that, perhaps, you are right and that you are not up to this task. As you can see, the mind and the thoughts on which you dwell are very powerful. Negativity is something your mind constantly has to contend with. The danger with negative thinking is how strong an influence it is and how much power it wields. Negative thinking is an example of a mindset that can break you. It's also the reason why some people find it difficult to make even the simplest of goals a reality while others are pushing boundaries and redefining their future. Feeding negative thinking can lead to a defeatist attitude, which in turn can move you to give up even before you've had a chance to begin.

Examples of the kind of habits that you need to train your mind to adopt include:

- The habit of persisting in the face of challenge.
- The habit of learning to control your impulses.

96

- The habit of learning to be flexible and adaptable with what you cannot control.
- The habit of thinking about your *thinking*.
- The habit of applying past knowledge to future circumstances.
- The habit of learning to communicate with clarity and precision to minimize the stress caused by miscommunication.
- The habit of learning to engage all your senses when trying to process the data you receive so you can control your emotions.
- The habit of learning to take responsible risks to create the change you want.
- The habit of learning to think interdependently.
- The habit of staying making learning a continuous and ongoing process.

Take control of your mind, because no one else will (or can) do it for you. It was Buddha who uttered the wise words, *each morning, we are born again, and what we do today matters most.* Reflect on those words for a moment and let it sink it. The sentence may be simple, but the impact left behind is powerful.

Habitual Mistakes That Cause Stress

Most of the time, a lot of the stress we feel has a lot to do with the poor habits we practice.

- **You're Procrastinating Too Much -** The number one bad habit and productivity killer. *Procrastination.* As far as bad habits go, this is about as tempting as they come, especially when you're not particularly fond of the task that you're supposed to be handling. When we have to deal with something we don't like, it can be tempting to keep pushing it back or putting it on hold because we don't want to do it. But that is exactly what stops you from being the master of your time. Even if you dread the task, the task is still there and eventually, you have to get around to doing it anyway, so why procrastinate?

- **Not Taking Breaks When You Need It -** Rushing to meet deadlines when you're running out of time means you're not taking the necessary breaks you need to recharge and manage your stress levels. Managing your time better doesn't mean working for 8 hours straight like a machine powering through all your tasks.

Not taking breaks when required is how you burn out quickly and that then becomes counterproductive because when you're burned out, it becomes harder to get back into focus and you lose time doing it. Whenever you've completed a task on your to-do list and you feel like you need a quick breather, go ahead and take it. Take a break, recharge, refocus your energy and then come back with renewed vigor to tackle the next task before you.

- **Ignoring the Distractions -** You waste a lot of time when you're distracted. Even if it is just for a minute or two because all those minutes add up. Phone calls, chats, texts, quick chats with colleagues, several coffee breaks in a day, all those add up and you suddenly realize that you've lost more time than you should in a day getting nothing done. Minimizing stress starts with eliminating all the distractions you currently have around you. This means your new habit needs to be removing *anything* that might even be potentially distracting your focus. Keep your phone on silent when you're working and commit to not letting any distractions take your attention away from what you're supposed to be doing. Take a break after you've completed a task, but avoid being distracted before.

- **Underestimating the Time You Need** - Another common pitfall that leads to a lot of stress is when you miscalculate the time and effort you are going to need to complete a particular task. The absence of realistic timelines is a habitual mistake that leads to a lot of unnecessary stress when you're scrambling at the last minute as you realize you're running out of time. What you should be doing instead is analyzing each task that you have in front of you and then set a realistic time frame for how long you would need to complete it. Don't set a timeline that *you think* should be the right one. Or a timeframe that you think you can squeeze through. Look at the task objectively and realistically decide how much time should be allocated to this task depending on how much work is going to be involved or how complicated the task is.

- **Focusing On the *Wrong* Things** - It's easy to make a lot of mistakes when you're stressed out and can't think clearly. Which means that another common habitual mistake that eventually leads to unnecessary stress is when you're focused on the wrong things. When you look at the task list that is in front of you, ask yourself if each and every one of those items is a task that is valuable, a task that is going to benefit you, and a task that is going to move you towards better goals. To make the most out of your time, and to make each moment a productive one, each task that you undertake needs to be tasks that are going to benefit you down the road. If it is in the workplace, each task should be one that is going to better your career and your skills as an employee that your company sees as a valuable member of the team.

How to Change Your Habits

Changing your habits can be a difficult thing to do, especially in the beginning. Making little changes to the way that you do things could be a bit of a struggle in the beginning, but don't be discouraged because it takes time for a new pattern of behavior to become a habit. Establishing a routine for yourself will make you a lot more productive. A routine allows you to get right down to the tasks that need to be done for the day, makes you more efficient because you know what needs to be done for the day without having to think too much about it, minimizes the time you need to spend on planning and helps to create structure in your life as well as instil good, productive habits when you do something in repetition. Having a familiar structure to your day like this minimizes the stress you feel too, even if you have a lot of things to do.

Here are some other strategies you can employ to help you change your habits:

- **Saying No When You Need To** - Maybe you don't like to do it, but you *have to do it.* You owe it to yourself to manage your stress levels and one way to do it is by learning to say no when you need to. There will be some moments when you need to say no. If you've already got too many things to focus on your plate right now, know when it is time to decline a request and you don't have to feel guilty about it. The tasks that you have on hand right now should be given attention and priority until they have been completed, and unless they are not marked important, if you already have your hands full, then learn to say no. Pile too much on your already full plate and you're going to increase your stress instead of eliminating it.

- **Forward Thinking and Planning - It** is always better to be well-prepared than to just wing it or go with the flow. If you find that leaving things to chance tends to elevate your stress levels, plan ahead as much as you can and take comfort in the knowledge that you're as prepared as you can be. You don't even have to go too far, by planning a week ahead of a month, maybe even a year ahead. Keep it simple by keeping it focused on planning for the next day. When you've got a lot of your task list to get through, planning your time wisely is an effective stress management approach. For example, when you've finished for the day at work, why not spend an extra 10-15 minutes clearing out your desk and preparing for tomorrow's task list by putting in on your desk so you're ready to go first time tomorrow morning. A simple, yet effective move.

- **It's Time to Make Yourself A Priority** - One habit you need to change is your tendency to neglect your self-care if that's something you've been guilty of for too long. As much as you want to try and do it all, you also need to remember to take care of yourself. Getting plenty of sleep, rest and exercise is how you maintain a mind that is sharp, alert and functioning well. So well that it can handle any challenge that comes along *without* feeling too much stress in the process.

- **Early to Bed, Early to Rise** - A common habit you'll notice among many successful individuals is how they make it a point to get up early in the morning. They start their day bright and early because they get to accomplish more.

They do more than most people do in a day, and if they're feeling the pressure, they've learned not to let it show because they've developed a series of good habits to help them cope. As long as you get 8-hours of sleep and you're fully rested, starting the day earlier than you usually could be the new habit that you need to minimize the stress you feel.

- **Having Buffer Time to Minimize Your Stress** - Begin this new habit called *buffer time*. Handling one task after another in a row with no break time is a one-way destination to burning out quickly. As much as you would quickly like to go through your task list and get everything done and over with as soon as possible, it is still important to give yourself time to recharge between each task by taking the needed breaks. This is called *buffer time*, and when scheduling your tasks for the day, it is important that you leave some buffer time in between to allow yourself to recharge your mental energy.

Developing the mental habits you need to become a more self-disciplined person is something everyone has within them to accomplish. There is no easy way or shortcut towards gaining more self-discipline and adopting better life habits that bring about the positive changes you want to see. You are going to have to put in the time, effort, and energy into the entire process if you want to make it happen. To become a disciplined person is going to require some sacrifices on your part. Adjustments need to be made, and there are going to be some difficult things you might have to do, but change is necessary for the greater good, and this must be a sacrifice you must be willing to make. Adopting the right habits is going to make you much tougher and stronger, more resilient towards obstacles and challenges, and you'll be a much better person at the end of this journey because of it. It is challenging, yes. Sticking to it and making this habit an integral part of your life is something that is going to take time. But if you are persistent, if you keep on going and get past the difficult hump, you will see just how worth it all the effort was when your life improves for the better.

Chapter 6: Relieve Anxiety

Humans have developed an automatic defense mechanism that has helped us survive for as long as we have. It is called the *fight or flight* response. In the face of danger, a person does either one of two things based on this response. We'll either turn and run the other way (*flight*) or we will face the challenge or danger head-on and try to confront it (*fight*). There's something else that happens too when we sense danger around us and when we're deciding what we should do. *We feel anxious.* The anxiety that we experience during these situations keeps our senses sharp. The early humans depended on this mechanism a lot before there was such a thing as big cities and safe places to live in. Those were the days when the anxiety felt was a lot simpler too and had only one purpose. To keep us safe.

These days, anxiety has morphed into something more complicated. At the slightest sign of perceived threat, we begin to worry. We worry about the bad things that may or may not happen. We worry about making it through the day unscathed by any disastrous episodes. We worry about meeting our deadlines for work and school. We worry about how we're going to save up enough money by the time we hit retirement. There's a lot to worry about and the kind of environment we live in today makes it easy for worries to become disproportionate. This means that it is more than likely the worry we feel does not match the perceived threat. If the worry lingers long enough and steadily gets worse, it's no longer worry anymore. It's *anxiety*. When your anxiety begins to get in the way of your daily functioning, you could be dealing with an anxiety disorder on your hands.

Understanding Severe Anxiety

Not a lot of people recognize that they have anxiety, let alone a case of severe anxiety. When we're anxious, the most common thing that is felt is the intense feeling of distress and worry.

The moment these emotions begin to feel like they're out of control, you're bordering dangerously close to severe anxiety territory. If you don't do anything about it, it quickly becomes a problem, stopping you from going about your day. Even simple challenges that should be easy become nearly impossible to manage when you've got severe anxiety.

Anxiety disorders have become a common problem today. Severe types of anxiety are often featured in a group of mental disorders that include:

- Generalized Anxiety Disorder (GAD)
- Social Anxiety Disorder (SAD)
- Post-traumatic Stress Disorder (PTSD)
- Obsessive-Compulsive Disorder (OCD)
- Panic Disorder
- Separation Anxiety Disorder
- Specific Phobias
- Agoraphobia

It is normal for everyone to experience anxious feelings from time to time (remember it's a built-in system that we have developed). Feeling nervous, jittery, and slightly concerned during the lead up to big moments, like having to give a speech, before a big test, starting a new job, or before the first date, for example, are normal. You might even say that in small doses, these emotions help us perform better because of how alert our senses become. Normal anxiety dissipates once the stressful moment is over, and we'll calm down as everything goes back to the way it was. At times, the worry may linger after the stressful moment has passed. Distress and fear creep in and if it lingers long enough, these emotions begin to gain momentum and strength. The stronger they get, the worse your emotions become until it develops into a case of severe anxiety.

You'll know the minute you've crossed over from regular anxiety to severe anxiety when you expect only the worse possible outcome from a situation and everything seems more alarming and dangerous than it is. Psychologists refer to this phenomenon as *catastrophizing*. The persistent worries that you feel begin to get in the way of your everyday living. Coping with work becomes hard, coping with school becomes hard, coping with social situations becomes hard, even getting out bed starts to feel hard. The danger with severe anxiety is how it can quietly develop so subtly over time that you don't notice the clues and the way it's affecting you. It's very likely someone else is going to notice the signs and symptoms way before you do. Unless they point it out, you could go for years without realizing you've got a very real anxiety problem that needs to be dealt with.

If you are concerned that your anxiety might be bordering on severe, these are the common indicators to keep an eye out for:

- You spend most of your time are worried or afraid.
- You spend more time being tense and on edge than relaxed.
- You start getting nervous or scared more easily than you used to.
- You're panicky and prone to frequent panic attacks lately.
- You're more agitated and irritable than ever.
- You genuinely worry that you might be going crazy.
- You feel disconnected from your body.

- You feel sick to your stomach (literally). There are times when you feel like you're going to throw up when you're worried.
- You begin to avoid social situations.

The frequent thoughts you have that might indicate the presence of severe anxiety include the following:

- "Everything always goes wrong I don't know what to do"
- "I can't handle my emotions anymore, it's getting to be too much"
- "I can't stay calm, I wish everything would stop"
- "I can't focus anymore"
- "I don't want to get out of bed today"
- "I wish I could escape from it all"

Other signs and symptoms you may be experiencing that indicate what you're dealing with might be severe anxiety include:

- Sleep difficulties, where you have trouble falling asleep and wake up frequently in between.
- A rapid heartbeat that feels like your heart is pounding against your chest.

- Profuse sweating or cold sweats.
- Feeling like you've got "pins and needles" in your joints.
- Upset stomach and digestive problems.
- Frequent headaches and migraines.
- Dizziness and nausea.
- Twitching and physically trembling when you're nervous.
- Difficulty concentrating.
- Feeling dehydrated and extremely thirsty all the time.
- Feeling overwhelmed and exhausted

Image Source: Betts Psychiatric

Anxiety Varieties

The term anxiety is used to describe a group of mental health conditions, with each disorder identified through a specific set of symptoms. It is absolutely possible for a person to experience more than one anxiety disorder category simultaneously. Aside from the common groups of anxiety disorders described above, other types that fall into the same anxiety category include:

- Selective mutism
- Substance-induced
- Medication-induced
- Anxiety from a certain medical condition

The factors that lead to the development of anxiety could relate to any number of the following:

- Family history (genetics)
- Personality
- Brain chemistry
- Traumatic life events
- Long-term stress
- A combination of any of these factors

Looking at The Major Anxiety Disorders

Anxiety disorders are a very serious condition that is not to be taken lightly. If left untreated, there's a real risk of anxiety developing into severe depression and eventually suicide when it feels like you can no longer take it anymore. Let's look at the major anxiety disorders that have been discussed in more detail:

Generalized Anxiety Disorder (GAD)

A person will be diagnosed with GAD by a medical expert or mental health professional if they experience intense periods of worry for more than six months. Intense worry in this context is more than just feeling nervous about an upcoming public presentation or right before an interview for a job you've been eyeing. The intense worry here is when the worries you feel persist and it encompasses several factors that you're worried about, not just a single thing anymore. The worries can grow so big in your mind that you're terrified from the minute you wake up in the morning and continue to worry for the rest of the day. Imagine having to deal with this worry every single day for the next six months or more. It's exhausting mentally, physically and emotionally.

Common causes of GAD worry could be anything from personal relationships, romantic relationships, finances, family, career or health issues. Sometimes you could worry about one thing at a time, and other times you worry about *all* of it together to the point the worry becomes overwhelming. It becomes difficult to do any of the things you normally do, like making a cup of coffee or walking to work. The symptoms of GAD that will be experienced on most days include:

- Intense worries that are hard to control
- Severe dread or chronic worry about several issues
- The daily routine is severely impacted by GAD
- Feeling restless and on edge all the time
- Getting fatigued, exhausted or tired easily
- Difficulty maintaining any kind of concentration (you can't even concentrate on a simple conversation that's happening in front of you)
- You feel like your mind goes blank a lot during the day
- Sleep difficulties because as soon as you close your eyes, you're plagued by worry

- Tense and sore muscles from the prolonged state of stress that your body is in.

If any of these symptoms sound familiar to you, it is important that you seek medical help immediately to determine if you do have GAD. Your doctor may prescribe several treatments based on the severity of your condition, including therapies like Cognitive Behavioral Therapy (CBT), medication and introducing several changes in your lifestyle.

Social Anxiety Disorder (SAD)
Alternatively referred to as social phobia, SAD is a condition that happens when a person becomes extremely afraid or terrified of any kind of social encounter. The main cause of that worry stems from a fear of being judged or ridiculed by others. SAD goes beyond feeling shy or nervous in passing when you're faced with a social situation. This is a more chronic condition and it will not go away on its own. Measures must be taken to overcome SAD or it is going to continue to affect several aspects of your life. Yes, it requires professional attention, that's how serious this condition is.

SAD's is going to affect your ability to function in the following situations:

- When you have to meet new people
- When you have to talk on the phone
- When you have to talk in front of others
- When you have to perform in public
- When you're being observed by others and all eyes are on you
- When you're eating out in public

For someone without SAD, those situations can be slightly nerve-wracking too. After all, it's never easy for some people to be in the spotlight. For those with SAD, this is magnified tense times over to the point they could become paralyzed by their fear.

You may be experiencing SAD if you relate to any of the following symptoms:

- You're intensely afraid or worry about being judged by other people
- You are afraid people will think poorly or negatively of you.
- You're afraid you're going to be rejected
- You're afraid you're going to do something to embarrass yourself in public.

- You actively avoid going to places where you know there is going to be a lot of people.
- You're significantly distressed when placed in a social situation.
- Your fear is palpable, and you start visibly shaking or trembling when you're in a social situation.
- You start sweating profusely and your face turns bright red from the blood rushing to it.
- Your mouth feels dry no matter how much you drink.
- Your heart is racing and it feels like your heart might beat right out of your chest.
- You lose the ability to speak coherently in a social situation that you end up stuttering or stumbling, only adding to the embarrassment you already feel.

Sometimes your fear over these social situations can be so intense that you:

- Worry until you make yourself physically sick.
- Worry for weeks or months before the event takes place.
- Worry that others are going to notice how terrified you feel and think poorly of you.

- Do everything you can to avoid having to go out in public.

SAD may be triggered by any of the following social-related instances:

- When you need to meet new people or meet authority figures
- When you're criticized by someone
- When you're in the spotlight and you know everyone is watching you.
- When you have to perform or speak in public.
- When you feel people watching your every move.
- When you feel embarrassed over something.

Those who are dealing with SAD know that what they're afraid of is irrational. They know it doesn't make sense to a lot of people, but they can't help the way they feel. Knowing that others think their fears are silly only makes them feel worse about themselves.

Several factors could contribute to the onset of SAD, including:

- Genetics
- Personality
- External environment
- Humiliating events previously encountered
- A history of being bullied or criticized.
- A history of sexual abuse.
- Personal conflicts with family.

SAD is a common disorder, and it is important that you seek the help you need to overcome the way you feel. Therapies like CBT can be immensely helpful in this situation. Anxiety is a very treatable condition, so don't despair too much because there is a way to overcome it.

Specific Phobias

This category of anxiety disorder is when a person experiences an irrational or strong fear of a specific situation or object. That person may try to avoid what they perceive as a threat and do everything they can to avoid contact, even when they may realize there is no real danger. Those with specific phobias feel at a loss and have no way of controlling their fear, and this phobia could become so intense that it affects their self-esteem and personal relationships. These phobias go beyond merely feeling nervous or anxious about flying or avoiding dogs because you're nervous they might bite you. Social phobias can cause extreme anxiety and reaction.

Examples of what common social phobias include:

- Fear of flying
- Fear of blood
- Fear of dentists
- Fear of spiders
- Fear of insects
- Fear of needles
- Fear of germs (being a germaphobe)
- Claustrophobia

The most common indicator of social phobia is a panic attack, although not everyone who deals with social phobia necessarily experiences a panic attack.

Symptoms of a panic attack include:

- Difficulty breathing (shortness of breath)
- Profuse sweating or cold sweats
- Feeling nauseous
- Difficulty talking

- Trembling and shaking

Like the other disorders so far, it is important to seek professional help if you're dealing with social phobias. You need to get the right kind of treatment if you want to overcome this form of anxiety disorder and it is impossible to try and do it alone.

Obsessive-Compulsive Disorder (OCD)

When you're feeling overwhelmed and you believe you're only going to feel better after you've performed a specific sequence of behaviors or rituals, that could be a sign you're dealing with OCD. Specific rituals or behaviors could be something like washing your hands three times after shaking hands with someone. Those who deal with OCD know that their fear may be irrational to others, but they *must* do it anyway or they won't be able to remain calm until they do. Dealing with OCD can cause you to worry about the same thing repeatedly, and the images or thoughts you run through your mind feed into your anxiety. OCD sufferers believe that only their "rituals" will bring relief for their anxiety. On some level, it will, but the relief is only temporary. The compulsive urge will soon return and you'll have to repeat the ritual over again.

The indicators of OCD could begin developing as early as childhood. These signs might go unnoticed for a long time before you or someone else starts to notice. Some signs that indicate you could be dealing with OCD include:

- Hands that are red and sore from repetitive washing.
- Difficulty touching anything in public.
- Difficulty shaking hands with others or experiencing any kind of contact.
- Reacting in an extreme manner when something does not go the way you planned.
- Repetitively checking on something, like having to check several times if you've turned off the light before you left the room (even though you did, and you've checked on it several times already).
- Difficulty accepting change in the routine and adapting to it.
- Difficulty getting to work on time because of your need to perform your "rituals".
- Repeating certain words or actions.

The trouble with OCD is it could occur alongside other health-related problems like drug abuse, eating disorders, alcohol consumption or depression, which makes it even harder to diagnose for sure. If you suspect you or someone you know might be dealing with OCD, get the help you need through the prescribed behavioral treatments that will help you deal with this condition. When you spend more than an hour or two on your rituals and have trouble getting through the day because your rituals either distract you or interrupt your routine, you need to seek help before it gets worse.

Panic Disorder
Recurring panic attacks are responsible for this anxiety disorder. Anything unexpected or overwhelming that happens to you can be a cause of intense distress or fear, triggering a panic attack in the process. Panic attack indicators are easier to spot than a lot of the other anxiety disorders, and they are:

- Difficulty breathing
- Racing heartbeat

- Chest palpitations and shortness of breath
- Dizziness and nausea
- Feeling numb all over from your fear
- You worry about the same thing for more than a month
- You start changing your behavior to avoid more panic attacks, possibly developing unhealthy coping mechanisms along the way.

It is common for people to experience a panic attack at some point in their lives. It only becomes a bonafide disorder when it happens too frequently and starts interfering with a lot of your daily routine. Those who deal with panic attacks frequently worry about the possibility of having *another* panic attack too, and this keeps them in a state of constant anxiousness. Sometimes the panic attacks could be so severe that medical help is needed, especially when there's shortness of breath in play.

Relaxing Your Body and Mind
Anxiety can be an emotionally, mentally and physically draining experience. The sooner you seek help, the better it will be. Often, a

combination of several factors is needed to help us get better if we're dealing with severe anxiety. This could involve getting the right help from a well-informed professional, undergoing the right kind of therapy, getting the support you need from family and friends, taking care of yourself through your diet and exercise routines, and finding new ways to manage your stress through self-help techniques like yoga and meditation.

Aim for methods that are going to help you specifically relax your mind and body, and it's not necessarily through yoga and meditation alone. What you need to start developing is the ability to think realistically. You will learn to develop this technique after a few sessions with your therapist. While it is hard to think positively all the time, what you need to work on changing is your tendency to view the world in a negative light as your first response. To avoid imagining the worst all the time, you need to develop the ability to think realistically. You need to look at all aspects of a situation, the good, bad and the neutral, and make a conclusion based on the facts you see. *Only the facts and nothing more.* In other words, you need to begin practicing the ability to see the world in a fair and balanced manner and to see things as they are.

Realistic thinking is developed by exercising the following techniques:

- **Monitoring the Way You Approach Self-Talk** - Watch the ongoing monologue that runs through your mind. Self-awareness about the nature of your self-talk is where you start making the necessary changes needed to change the way you think. If you're undergoing CBT therapy as part of your recovery, this is going to be a big part of how you change your mindset.

- **Pinpoint the Unhelpful Thoughts** - Distinguish the unhelpful thoughts from the negative ones. Not all negative thoughts are necessarily bad. An example of a negative thought is *"I'm stressed and frustrated, but I know it will get easier"* while an unhelp thought would be *"I hate my current job and I never want to go back to that office again!"*. The unhelpful thoughts are the ones you want to focus on getting rid of.

- **Challenge Your Thoughts** - Once you've identified what your unhelpful thoughts are, it's time to work on challenging them. If they're not valid and based on facts, push back against these thoughts by focusing on the information that you know. Replace these unhelpful thoughts with concrete facts to support your argument and make it believable. The facts never lie and focusing on this is one way of reigning in your thoughts to keep them from spiraling out of control.

Chapter 7 - Eliminate Negative Thinking

Your inner critic is your own worst enemy. We all have a nasty little inner critic that lives somewhere in our mind and if we let it out, listen to it and start to believe everything that it tells us, we're in big trouble. Sometimes the little voice in your head can be helpful if your mindset is one that knows how to use this voice as motivation to make changes for the better. Like when your inner critic reminds you junk food is not good, or that you need to get up and start exercising if you want to look good at the family wedding next month. But sometimes, the little voice takes a nasty turn and does more harm than good, especially when it starts steering us towards the realm of excess negativity. When this happens, what we're engaging in is negative self-talk and if you let it, it will bring you down so low you'll find yourself drowning in negativity with no help in sight.

Negative self-talk. Everyone experiences it from time to time and when it happens, it doesn't just bring a dark cloud of negativity with it. It causes significant stress to us and the people around us if we're not careful about it. If you have dreams, goals, and desires, then it is about time to start doing yourself a favor and make it happen. You owe it to yourself to live every day as the best version of yourself. You have everything that you need to begin, all it takes is a mere shift and change in the way that you think. It is now up to you to use that and start transforming your life into what you want it to be.

Understanding Negative Thinking and Self-Talk

Negative thinking is not present all the time. Usually, these harmful, self-deprecating thought patterns manifest during times of immense stress or when you're faced with a particularly challenging situation. During those moments, any negative thought tendencies you have will probably be magnified, eventually leading to anxiety, overthinking, reinforcing all the worst ideas you believe about yourself. Because a lot of these beliefs are developed over time, they're almost habitual which means they can become very difficult to change. Defeatist thinking like this is the biggest reason many fail to reach the goals they have set, because the challenges, the setbacks, disappointments, and failure can often strip you of the will you need to keep going. If you don't have the needed resilience, it won't be long before those challenges eventually get to you and you give up on your goals.

Image Source: The Best Brain Possible

Obstacles are not easy to overcome. If you've ever looked at other successful individuals who have made it and wondered how they got to where they are, you're not alone. How did they overcome the challenges, rise above the odds without ever feeling like they wanted to give up? How did they have such will and desire to make it through to the end? What was it that propelled them to achieve their desires? Persevering against everything that was designed to bring them down? Everyone wants to know how they did it. We may not know the full story and distinctive factors contributed to their success, but the one thing we *do know* is that they didn't do it with negative thinking and self-talk.

The musings of your inner critic can sometimes sound like a critical friend or family member who admonishes you. Negative self-talk can come in several versions. It some versions, it sounds grounded. For example, when you say *"I'm not the best at this task, so perhaps I should let someone else take charge so we don't compromise the outcome."* In other versions, it can sound downright cruel or mean, like when you say, *"I can never do anything right! I should just give up!"*. It could even sound like you're realistically appraising the situation when you say, *"I didn't get an A on my science test again, I guess I'm not good at science after all,"* although this version could quickly morph into fantasies based on fear, such as *"I'll probably never get into college if I keep scoring low grades on my tests like this!".*

Like negative thinking, critical self-talk follows the path of cognitive distortions, where you blame, catastrophize, and hate yourself for what you perceive as your shortcomings. Keep this up and you'll quickly diminish the possibility of making any kind of positive change in your life because your self-esteem and confidence will be so far gone you'll need some serious damage control to get back on track. The challenges you are going to face along the way throughout your life can quickly drain you and make you feel burned out. It is important that you keep your motivation and your spirits high to stay on track towards achieving any goal that you have. Where do you get started? By changing your mindset to eliminate negativity and the negative self-talk that goes along with it. If you are tired and discontent with living a life of mediocrity, it is time to stop wishing things would get better and start doing something about it. Nothing is going to change unless you do, and right here is where you start – *by getting rid of negativity* and breaking free of its cycle once and for all.

Possible Causes of Negative Thinking and Self-Talk

It is hard to say for certain what us to think this way or why we still choose to engage in negative talk that only makes us feel even worse about ourselves. Pinpointing the exact cause is tricky, but there is a possibility that negative thinking and self-talk is a combination of both environmental factors and life experiences. That the way we think could contribute to the development of our poor self-talk habits and bleak perception of life. How? Take for example how socially anxious people tend to think and *overthink* how they will perform poorly in social situations. They keep on thinking, and thinking, and thinking and going over and over again in their minds how everyone will be paying close attention to them and scrutinizing their every move. They think that people are constantly observing what they're doing and saying. These negative beliefs will eventually come to affect them if they keep obsessing about it often enough, and this could eventually lead to high levels of social anxiety experienced by the person.

The experience we go through can leave an impact so deep the memories stay with us forever. If someone previously experienced fear and humiliation in a similar situation, they may worry about it occurring again and as a result, they eventually become fearful of experiencing a repeat of this situation. Young children, for example, who experience bullying, teasing, humiliation, rejection, ridicule and more may be more prone to developing negative thinking and self-talk because of the influence they received from this experience as they progress into adulthood. Other negative events such as family conflict and sexual abuse could also play a part in a person's negative perception and the way they look at life in general. It is only natural to want to avoid and stay away from things that we do not want to do. If a situation is going to bring out nothing but feelings of fear, discomfort, anxiety and sheer panic, you are going to want to do everything you can to get away from that situation or avoid it altogether.

Anyone who is plagued by negative thoughts and self-talk they can't escape from must learn to recognize what these negative thoughts are doing to them. These negative thoughts are impacting your life and it's time you start taking some serious action. You are the only person who can overcome this because you're the one going through it, and acceptance begins with you.

Indicators It's Time to Change Your Thinking

Negative thinking can cause a lot of emotional reactions that are neither productive nor helpful in remedying the situation. Yes, something unexpected happened, but you need to be able to view it in an objective way if you're going to find a solution to overcome the problem. Letting your negative thoughts and self-talk rule the day is only going to set you back further and further. The more you slide backward, the harder it will be to get back on track since a lot more effort needs to be put into it. Staying calm and staying focused is how you hone in on the resilience that is already within you.

Your thoughts are a part of who you are, and there's no running away from it. Your thoughts can hurt you more than you know. The problem with a negative mindset is that it acts like an anchor that weighs you down, and while it may be hard to overcome, it is not impossible. The problem is, not everyone recognizes the indicators that tell them something needs to be done. Our minds send us red flag warnings all the time. The question is, do we know how to recognize them?

Indicator #1 - Unhappiness Seems to Be A Permanent State

A negative mindset will blind you to all the good things you have going on in your life. Seeing and staying positive daily becomes a challenge for you. Your mindset seems to be acting as an anchor, and the more you dwell on it, the further into despair you find yourself sinking. No matter how many good things you have to be grateful for, you find yourself feeling unhappy and miserable all the time, which eventually strips you of any desire or ambition to grow and develop yourself.

Indicator #2 - You're Either Tired or You're Demotivated

Lacking any desire to do anything is a clear sign that your negative mindset is starting to get to you. When even the simple pleasures in life start to feel like a chore, that's an indication that you've got to change before you lose all desire to even leave the house anymore. Negative thinking leaves you drained, tired and demoralized all the time because nothing feels like it is worth the effort. Have many times have you found yourself guilty of bailing out on plans and canceling activities because you "didn't feel like it?" If you answered far too often or more than you would have liked, now you know why. If you find yourself lacking a zest for life, it's a sure sign that something needs to change and quick.

Indicator #3 - Relationships Feel Like A Challenge

Constant negative self-talk and criticism are going to damage your self-esteem and confidence in the long run. By the time you start paying any attention to the way you're affected, your relationships have already suffered the effects of poor communication. No one likes being around a complainer or someone who is down in the dumps all the time, no matter how much they love you. It's emotionally exhausting to be around someone who complains or has nothing positive to say. Even when they try to cheer you up, your automatic response is to counter it with a negative statement. Negativity is a draining emotion, and there's only so much a person can talk before they've reached their limit.

Indicator #4 - Your Professional Life Begins to Suffer from Limited Thinking

This is probably going to be the biggest setback in your professional life. To think that nothing will change and anything you do is just setting yourself up for another disappointment is a tell-tale sign that you need to change your mindset. Believing that you "can't do it" is going to stop you from trying at all, and the minute you don't try is the moment you've lost already. If you don't do something to change the way you think and quick, it will do nothing except deplete your energy and bring down your self-esteem, stopping you from achieving what you are truly capable of. You always have the power to change your situation, and it's time to kick this belief out the door if you want to truly change your mindset and start transforming your life.

Indicator #5 - You're Defined By Your Complaints and Self-Criticism

Remember how emotionally draining it can be to be around a complainer? You've probably crossed paths with a few complainers in your life, and that will give you some idea of what it's like to be on the receiving end. Self-awareness needs to be practiced here as you try to think about whether you're complaining about the same old thing all too often. Do you find that all you seem to be doing is complaining about them but not doing anything to change or make it better? If you find yourself doing this, it is high time you

start changing your mindset for the better, because no good will ever come out of complaining except to drive a wedge between you and the people who are close to you. Criticizing yourself for your shortcomings is not going to be of much help either. Everyone has the power within them to change for the better, more power than they realize. Nothing is ever set in stone, and once you change your mindset, you'll see just how many other doors of opportunities begin to open up.

Indicator #6 - Excuses, Excuses

There's always going to be a reason not to do something. You prefer to make excuses rather than make an actual effort to change and you find yourself being put-off by people who try to suggest doing things differently. That's something negative thinking will make you good at. That's because you don't have the right kind of mindset that is needed to achieve success. Negative thinking stops you from seeing the opportunities and possibilities of a challenge. All you can see are the reasons why it isn't going to work or

Succeed. Finding reasons *not* to do something. There's always going to be a reason if you're looking for it, that's the rule of thumb you need to remember from now on.

Eliminating Negative Thinking for Good

If your current thoughts are not a reflection of who you want to be, then it is time to change them. That is the only way to start improving your life. When your thoughts in the deepest part of your subconscious don't coincide with your actions, that's when you find life becomes a struggle. That's when the negative vibes start to come pouring in. You need to unload your mind from all the negative energy that you've been carrying around with you all this time.

- **No More Dwelling on The Past -** Mistakes happen, nothing can go perfectly 100% of the time. Learning to let go of past mistakes that have happened isn't always easy, but it is something that must be done if you want to reshape your mindset and change your thought patterns. You need to start each day anew, with a fresh round of determination and tell yourself "today is a new day, and I will make it better than the last!". When you treat each day as a new opportunity, it reawakens your motivation and your passion to make each day even better than the last. You can then use this fuel to your advantage by feeding it with positive affirmations to make it even stronger than ever.

- **No More Overthinking -** The more we think about the negative challenges that are in our way, the worse it seems to become. Worrying and overthinking are two factors which have never helped anyone get very far in life, and only serve to weaken your resolve and resilience if you keep feeding into it. Our minds have a way of building things up and blowing it out of proportion if we dwell on it long enough because it gets entangled in our web of emotions, and suddenly something that is doable seems like the most impossible thing in the world. Don't overthink the obstacle you're facing, but instead view it from an objective point of view and learn to see it for what it is.

Don't embellish, don't assume, and don't overanalyze it, just look at it based on facts.

- **Trade Negativity for Optimism -** Admittedly, it can be hard to remain positive all the time, especially when you've experienced a setback or things are not going according to plan. Since people are unique, there is no one-size-fits-all solution in this instance, what makes one person happy might not necessarily work for someone else. If you are going to maintain the motivation you need to keep going, it is very important that you find a way to stay positive, no matter what obstacles you may face. Setbacks can sometimes be opportunities in disguise, just like failures can be the best kind of teacher. It all depends on how you look at it. What you could do instead is try to look at each setback as a learning opportunity, and train your mind to look at this from a positive point of view. See the bright side and the good of every situation, and you will find that often the situation may not be as bleak as it initially seems.

- **Affirmations to Give You A Purpose** - When was the last time you set a goal for yourself that you were determined to reach and not back down no matter what challenges were thrown your way? If it has been far too long, then it's time for things to change. Here is where *positive* self-talk and *positive* affirmations are critical to helping you change your thought patterns. Take the negative thoughts that you have now and think about what you can do to turn these thoughts around. How do you switch from negative to positive? They can be the mighty force that gives you a purpose, and when your mind has something to focus on, everything in your life will start to align towards making it happen.

- **Assess Your Obstacles** - When we don't know what we're up against, it becomes harder to overcome. Analyzing the obstacles in your path to success is part of the process to overcome your negative thinking. Know your "enemy" and understand what you're dealing with so you're mentally able to better prepare to face it head-on. When you know what you need to do, that alone can help to strengthen your resolve to see something through. It helps to have a list of priorities on hand too.

- **List Your Priorities** - When an obstacle hits and throws all your plans in chaos, it's easy to get swept up in an emotional negative storm if you have nothing to fall back on. Being unable to identify what your priorities are will only serve to make the situation worse than it actually may be. To make sure that doesn't happen to you, you need a list of priorities. When you start on a goal, make a list of priorities that accompany that goal, and when you lose sight of that, whip out the list again to help you regain some clarity and focus, and tell yourself *I can do this!* Your inner critic may try to silence you and hold you back along the way, but with a list of priorities in hand that reminds you of what you want to accomplish, you've got the emotional support system you need to keep you staying in control.

- **Learning to Believe in Yourself Again -** You can be surrounded by all the positivity in the world, but if you don't *believe* in yourself and your abilities, you're not going to go very far either. Part of becoming a more resilient person is believing in yourself, after all, you've made it this far haven't you? You wouldn't have if you weren't already a capable person.

No matter what difficulties or challenges life may through at you, remember you have the power – *and now the techniques* – within you to help you get through it. In life, relationships or work, challenges are a constant part of our life and there will always be another challenge and another obstacle to face. But you always have a choice of how you want to react to it. That's the beauty of being human, we can do absolutely anything we set our minds to. It's not going to be easy, but it can be done, and that's what you need to keep reminding yourself each time you struggle to get past your inner critic.

Conclusion

Thank you for making it through to the end of *Eliminate Stress*, let's hope it was informative and able to provide you with all of the tools you need to achieve your goals whatever they may be.

A life that is completely free of stress may not always be possible. At some point, we need a little bit of stress to respond to the challenges we need to face. The light enough of a fire under us so we get moving and get things done. Without it, we would become far too complacent and probably not a lot of progress would be made. If you think about it, every tech application, appliance, gadget, and modern-day convenience we have was born in some ways because of stress. Everything we have today is designed to make our lives *easier* so that logically, we would have less stress to contend with. So yes, some amount of stress is necessary.

The point of this book was to hopefully show you that a lot of the stress you probably deal with today is unnecessary. Like when you worry about what you can't control. That's unnecessary because it's not going to change the outcome. Or when you worry about the past or future. Much of the stress we deal with today could be handled a lot better with the right coping strategies, time management and, of course, eliminating the need for worrying excessively. Learning to overcome and manage your stress is not going to happen overnight, but if you keep practicing every piece of advice you've learned from this book, you're doing much better than you were yesterday.

Finally, if you found this book useful in any way, a review on Amazon is always appreciated!

CPSIA information can be obtained
at www.ICGtesting.com
Printed in the USA
BVHW061359250221
601119BV00006B/554